THE OLD TESTAMENT MADE SIMPLE

THE

OLD

TESTAMENT

MADE

SIMPLE

By Melton Short

WORLD IMPACT MINISTRIES
P.O. BOX 412 CLANTON, AL 35046
☎ (205) 280-0999

CONTENTS

PREFACE

It has been estimated that less than 10% of all church people have a good, thorough understanding of the overall structure and framework of the Old Testament. Several years ago, I became quite concerned about this. Suddenly, an idea occurred to me which I immediately knew could totally revolutionize a person's ability to grasp and understand the Bible--and the Old Testament in particular.

Very soon, many other ideas came; and I have developed them into what you are about to read, THE OLD TESTAMENT MADE SIMPLE.

In this book you will go through the Old Testament eight different ways, each of which is a structure and framework within itself. As soon as you make your first trip, you will have a "skeleton" or framework **on which to continue building.** Each remaining trip simply adds to, strengthens, and further develops that framework.

My goal is that once you have completed this book **you will be able in total darkness to go through the entire Old Testament in skeleton form.** This certainly does not mean that you will know all that you need to know, **but you will have** a skeleton that you can put as much "meat" on as you choose to for the rest of your life. From that point onward, you will find that **every hour of Bible study and every Old Testament sermon that you hear will be greatly multiplied in value to you.**

You will, of course, still have to depend on the Holy Spirit to divinely illuminate the Word to you. This is simply information that God can use to do His mighty work in your heart.

It is my prayer that as you read, the Old Testament will become very clear and plain to you and that this study will be one of the most rewarding experiences of your entire life.

Eight Quick And Easy Ways To Get A Clear-Focused Overview Of The Entire Old Testament

STEP NUMBER 1:

THE SEVEN MAJOR MOVES OF THE PEOPLE OF THE OLD TESTAMENT

THE SEVEN MAJOR MOVES OF THE PEOPLE OF THE OLD TESTAMENT

During their 4,000 year history, the people of the Old Testament made **seven major geographical moves; and it is absolutely incredible how clear-focused the entire Old Testament can become simply by knowing these seven moves in sequence, why each move was made, the circumstances surrounding it, and how each one fits into God's overall plan.** This one thing by itself will give you a good, broad picture of the Old Testament.

BUT FIRST. . . . . .

Before we look at the seven moves themselves, **let me give you a quick and simple way to become familiar with the land of the Bible.** Let's start by stripping away everything except the bare essentials which will give you a "skeleton view" of the entire area.

Since the whole world has recently become acquainted with the Persian Gulf and since Abraham's hometown of Ur is only a few miles north of there, **I would like to use the Persian Gulf as a beginning point.**

As you know from the recent Gulf war, the Persian Gulf is on the east side of a "big-time" desert that covers thousands of square miles. Surrounding that huge desert on the north, east, and west sides, there is a **narrow stretch of very fertile land** that is shaped in the form of a crescent, or semi-circle. This stretch of land is known as **The Fertile Crescent**, and **almost every single thing** that you read about in the Old Testament took place **either inside or very near** this narrow stretch of land!!!

The Fertile Crescent extends northward from the Persian Gulf for approximately 600 miles. Then forming a semi-circle (crescent) it extends west and then southward along the coast of the Mediterranean Sea through the land of Israel and into the country of Egypt.

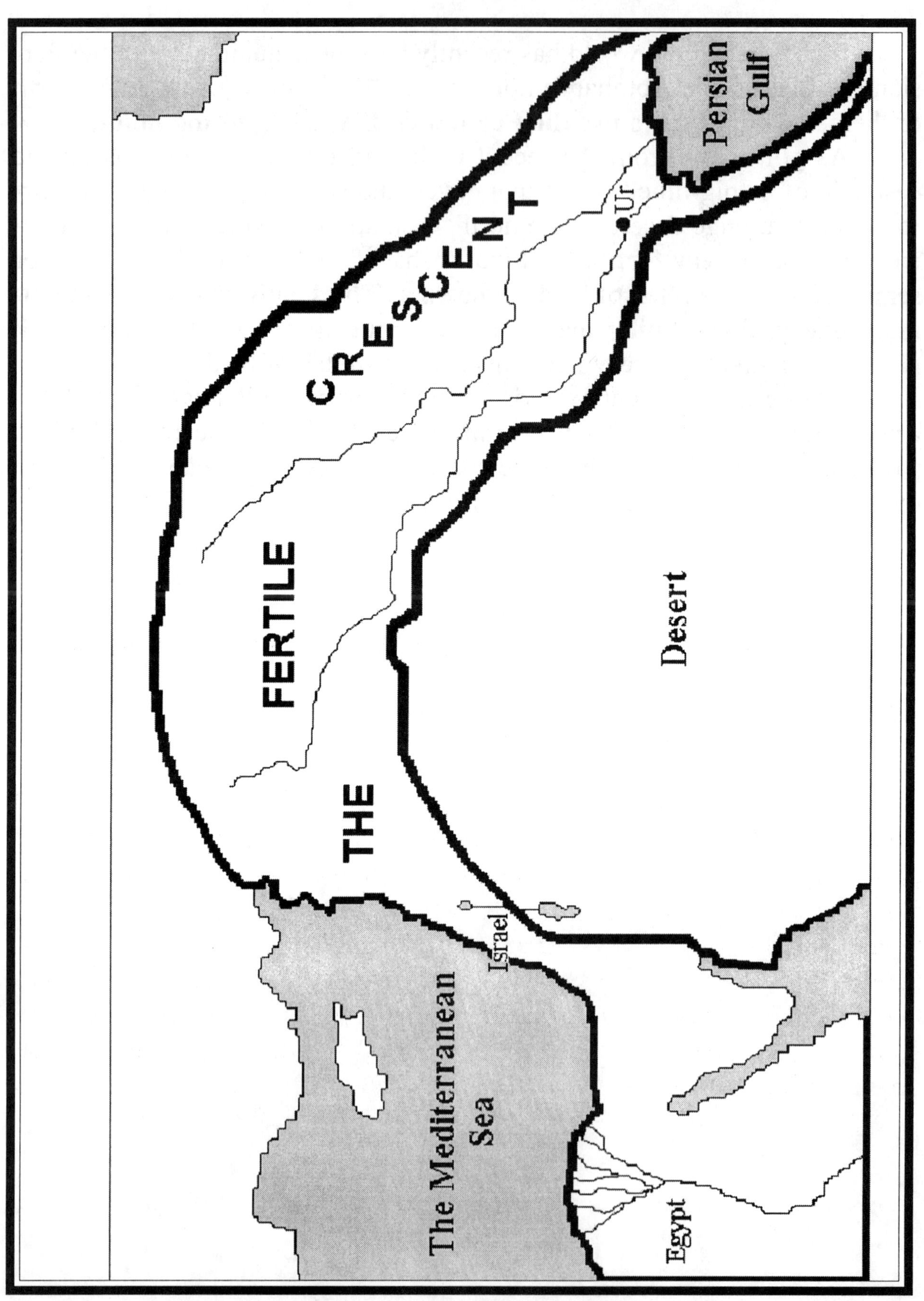

THE FERTILE CRESCENT
Persian Gulf
Ur
Desert
Israel
The Mediterranean Sea
Egypt

Notice the map on the previous page which shows each of the places that I have named, and let's zero in and examine each of these places to be sure that you have their location firmly fixed in your mind.

1. **The Persian Gulf.**

2. **Ur** -- Abraham's hometown just north of the Persian Gulf.

3. **The Desert** -- to the west of the Persian Gulf and to the east of Israel and Egypt.

4. **The Fertile Crescent** -- the narrow band of land forming a semi-circle and surrounding the desert on the north, east, and west sides. It is very important to remember that almost every single thing you read of in the Old Testament took place either inside or very near this narrow stretch of land.

5. **The Mediterranean Sea.**

6. **Israel** -- the narrow country on the coast of the Mediterranean Sea.

7. **Egypt** -- slightly southwest of Israel.

These few places are **enough** to frame together the entire region, yet the number of places is **small enough** that you will be able to get a crystal clear "picture" in mind within minutes. **And once you have that good "skeleton view" to work from, you will find that NEW places will just "drop in place" almost by themselves.** Before long you will have added many other places to your memory bank, and you will begin to find that Old Testament stories and events are **becoming far more meaningful** to you and are **far easier to remember simply because you will then be able to "picture" the setting** for those events in your mind.

There are just a few more places that you need to know, and then you will be able to trace **every one of the major moves** made by the people of the Old Testament.

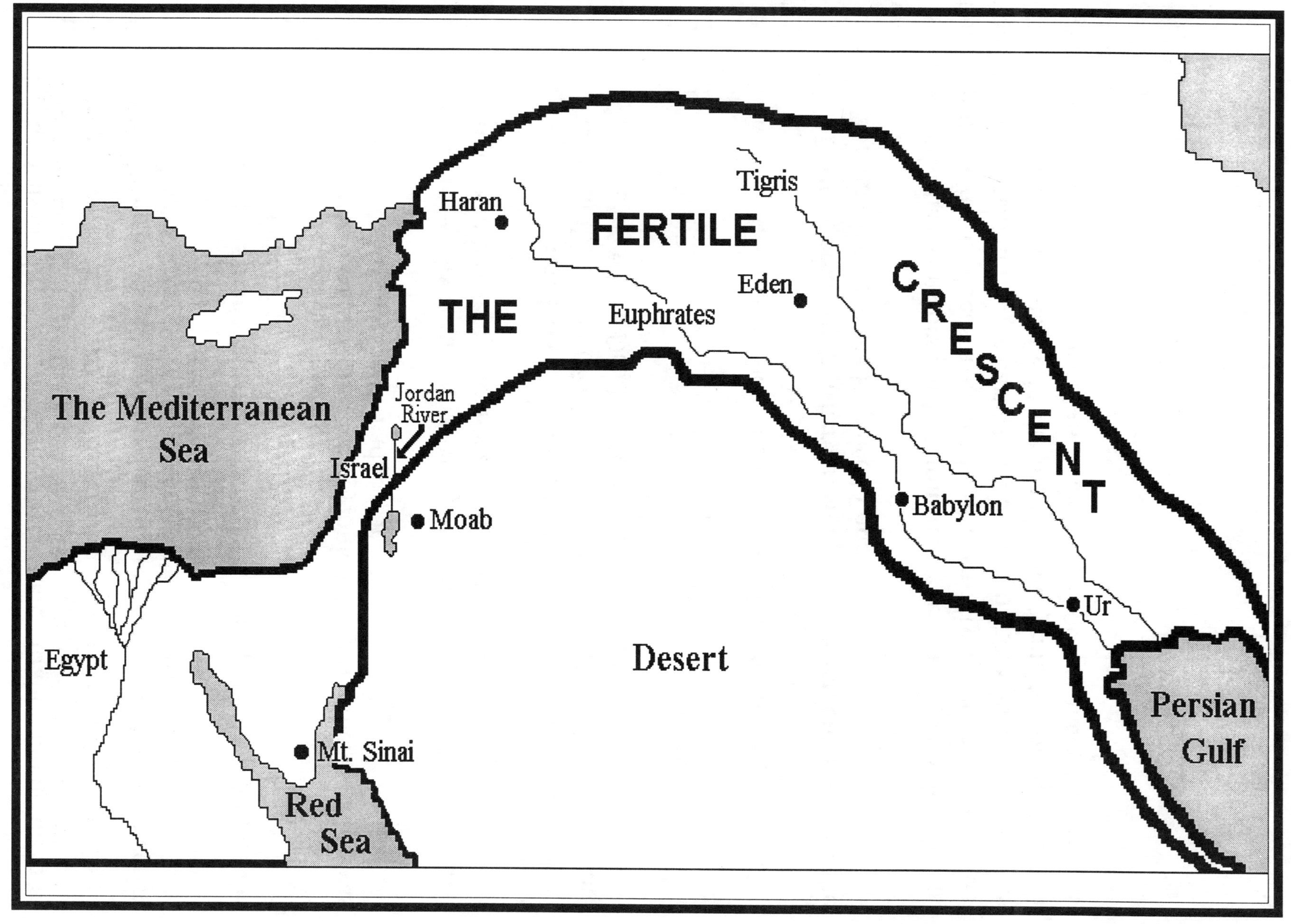
The Mediterranean Sea
Egypt
Red Sea
Mt. Sinai
Israel
Jordan River
Moab
THE FERTILE CRESCENT
Haran
Euphrates
Tigris
Eden
Desert
Babylon
Ur
Persian Gulf

Let's focus on the places that have been added to the map on the previous page.

1. **Eden** -- no one knows for sure where Eden was; but from scriptural references, the approximate place is known.

2. **The Tigris and Euphrates** -- two important rivers north of the Persian Gulf.

3. **Babylon** -- capital of the Babylonian Empire where Judah was carried captive by Nebuchadnezzar.

4. **Haran** -- city at the northern point of the Fertile Crescent that figures into several Old Testament stories.

5. **The Jordan River** -- the crooked river winding southward through the nation of Israel. (Note also the Sea of Galilee at the north end and the Dead Sea where the river ends).

6. **The Red Sea.**

7. **Mt. Sinai** -- place where the Law was given to Moses.

8. **Moab** -- point from where Joshua led the Israelites across the Jordan River into the Promised Land.

I suggest that you spend a **few minutes every few days** looking at this map **until these places are firmly and solidly in your mind.** After you have this small amount clearly fixed in your mind, you can add to it as little or as much as you desire in the months and years to come. You will have a foundation to build on. Now, let's take a look at the seven moves themselves.

MOVE NUMBER 1:

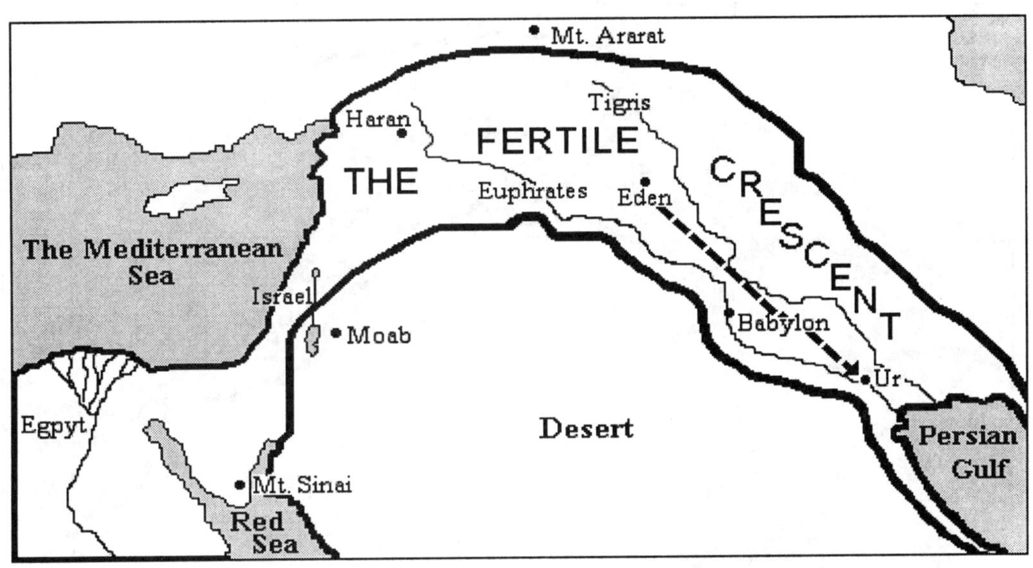

EDEN TO UR

The first move would obviously be **from EDEN to somewhere,** because that is where it all began. After Adam and Eve sinned, God drove them out from the beautiful garden that He had prepared for them. Over the years as man began to multiply, they gradually migrated southward within the fertile region toward the Persian Gulf. Later, when the flood came and destroyed all but eight people, the ark came to rest on Mt. Ararat (see map above). But once again they migrated southward where they had been before. In fact, there were some major population shifts after the flood that took them even farther south all the way to **UR** and even beyond.

MOVE NUMBER 2:

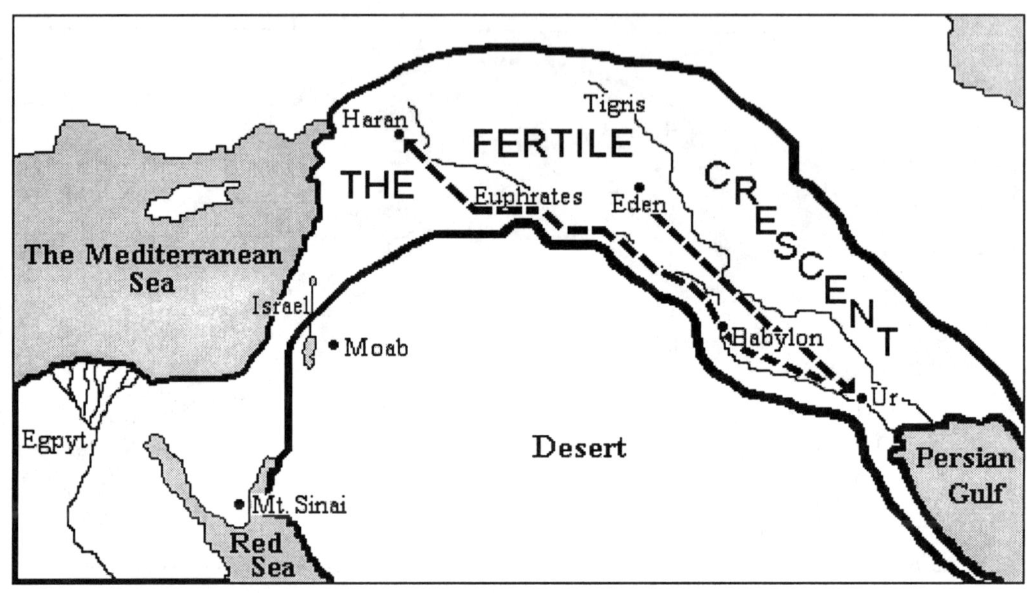

UR TO HARAN

One of the real focal points of scripture is God's appearance to Abraham in the land of **UR** at which time God gave him two promises. He promised to make a mighty nation of Abraham and to "bless all families of the earth" through his seed. God commanded him "Get thee out of thy country . . . . unto a land that I will show thee."

Move number two was the initial part of this command. Abraham did not go all the way into this "promised land" immediately; but he did leave **UR** and moved to **HARAN** where he stayed until his father, Terah, died.

MOVE NUMBER 3:

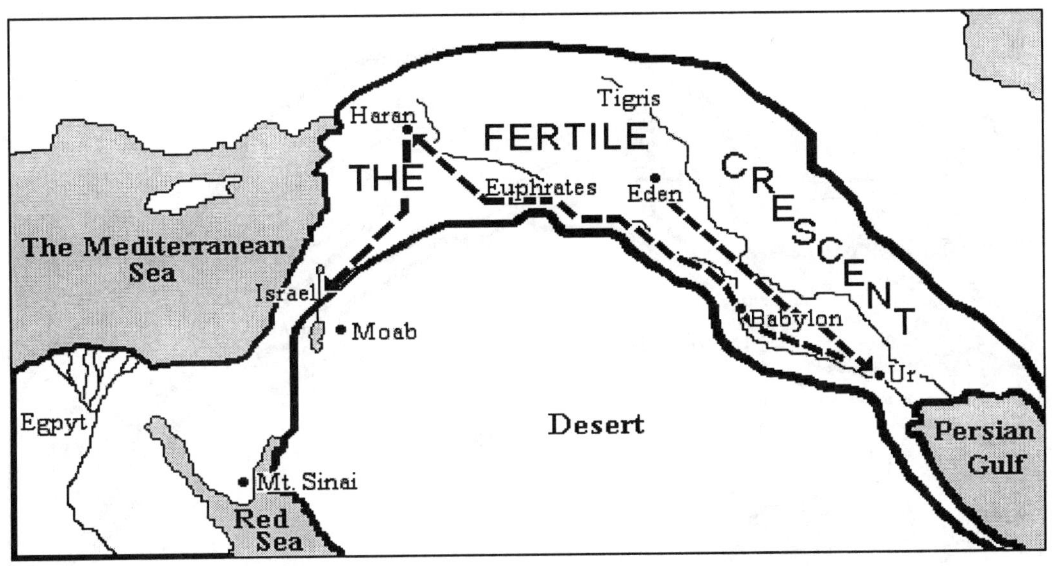

HARAN TO ISRAEL

After Abraham's father, Terah, died, God renewed the commission; and Abraham moved from **HARAN** on into **ISRAEL.** Once there, this "nation" that God had promised to make of Abraham began to grow. It had been twenty-five years since the promise had been given, but finally Isaac was born; **and the "nation" that God had promised was "on its way."** For the time being, the only thing in **sight** was a seven-pound baby (or whatever Isaac weighed); but Abraham believed God and knew that a "mighty nation" would spring forth from that one child. **And it did!!**

MOVE NUMBER 4:

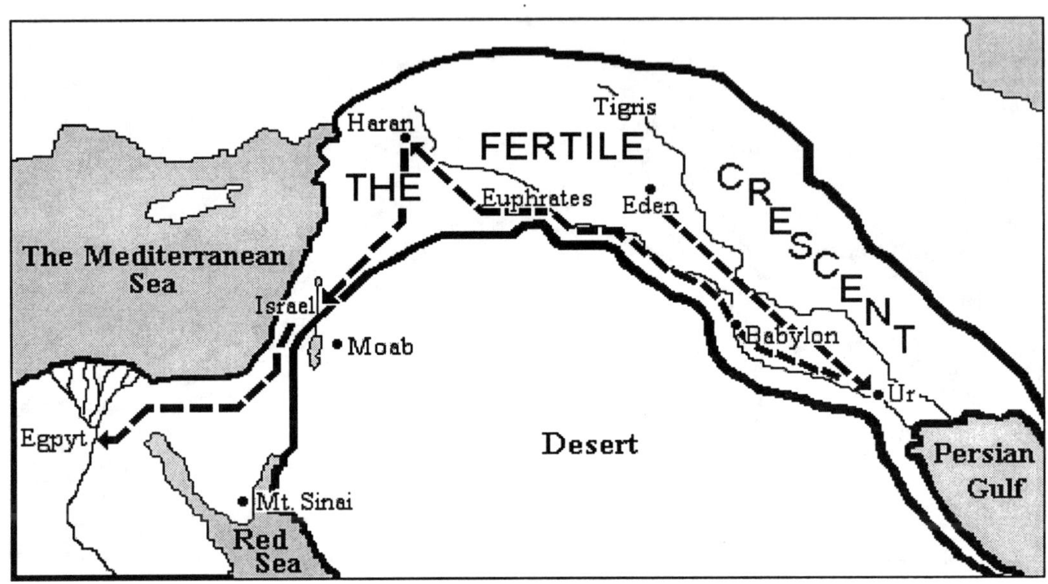

ISRAEL TO EGYPT

The fourth major move was from **ISRAEL** to **EGYPT**. This move **began** when Joseph was sold by his brothers to Midianite merchantmen who carried him to Egypt. This was clearly an act of God that would have long-range consequences. God blessed Joseph, and after a time brought him in contact with Pharaoh. Pharaoh had a dream which Joseph interpreted. The dream warned of a seven-year famine that would soon come. Joseph not only interpreted the dream but he also told Pharaoh what should be done. Pharaoh took Joseph's instructions; and during the seven years of plenty that preceded the famine, corn was stored in abundance.

After the famine came, the storehouses were opened. Back in Israel, Joseph's family heard that there was corn in Egypt and came to buy. The story of Joseph's gracious treatment of his brothers who had treated him so cruelly and who had sold him into Egypt is one of the most beautiful stories of the entire Bible. He freely forgave them and told them, **"it was not**

you that sent me hither, **but God."** Joseph then had his father and the entire family brought to Egypt where they could be cared for during the famine. Although the original purpose of the move was for them to only be there during the famine, this was a move that lasted for more than 400 years.

MOVE NUMBER 5:

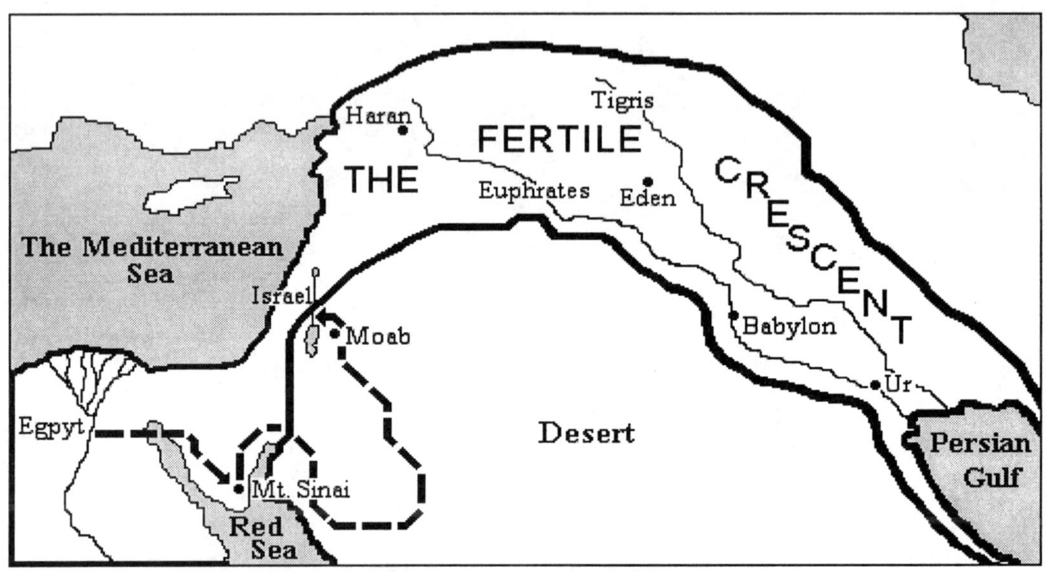

EGYPT BACK TO ISRAEL

For a time, Joseph's family was treated royally and given the best of the country; but as generations passed, **"there arose a (Pharaoh) who knew not Joseph."** Suddenly things drastically changed. The Egyptians became fearful that this "foreign nation" that was multiplying so rapidly within their borders might in a time of invasion turn and fight against them. So they began to greatly oppress and suppress the Israelites. This oppression grew worse and worse and the people began praying fervently for deliverance. God answered that cry and raised up Moses to deliver them from what had now become strong Egyptian bondage.

Through many signs and miracles, God miraculously delivered them; and they left **EGYPT** to return to **ISRAEL**. This move took 40 years to complete, but after the 40 years of wilderness wanderings they arrived back in their "promised land."

MOVE NUMBER 6:

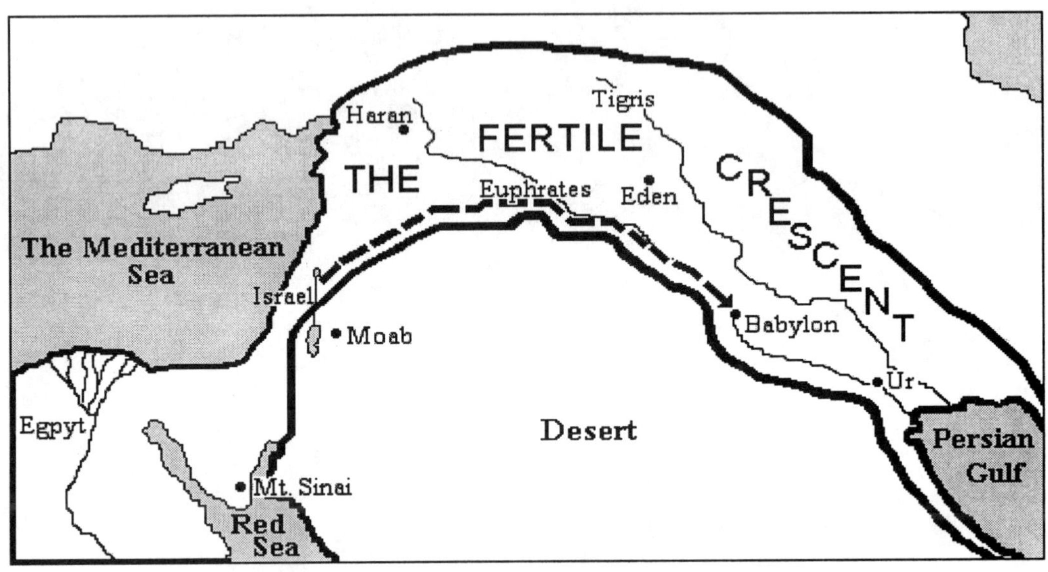

ISRAEL TO BABYLON

The sixth major move came approximately 1,000 years later when Nebuchadnezzar came and carried large groups captive to **BABYLON** where they remained in exile for the next 70 years.

MOVE NUMBER 7:

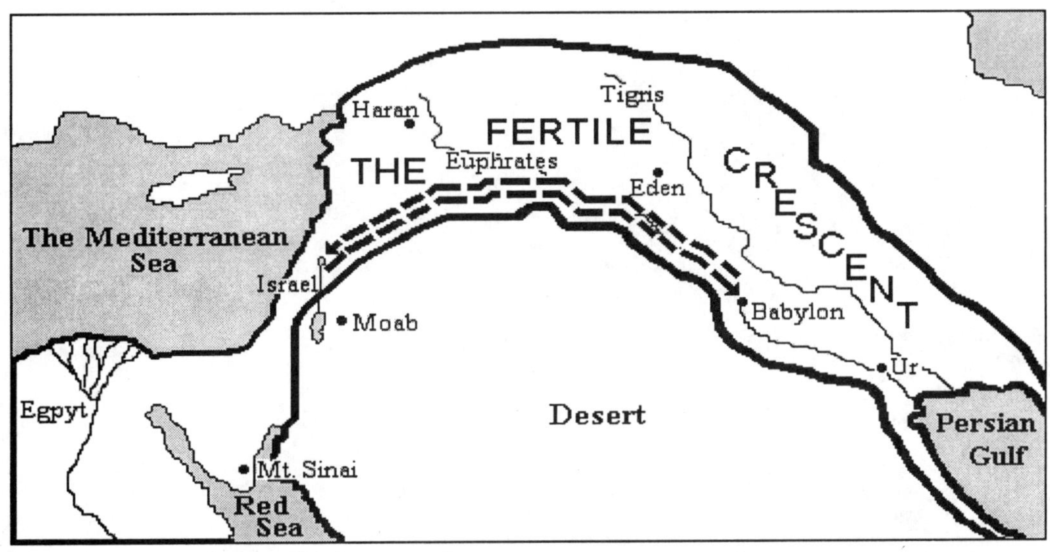

BABYLON BACK TO ISRAEL

The seventh and final move was from **BABYLON** back to **ISRAEL**. Before Judah was taken captive, the prophets had not only warned them that unless they repented and turned back to God they would be carried into captivity; but they had also told them that after 70 years of exile God would restore them to their homeland.

As the 70th year neared, God allowed the Babylonian kingdom to be overthrown by the Persians. The Persians' concept of world conquest differed from that of the Babylonians; and Cyrus, the king of the Persians, allowed them to return to Jerusalem "right on time" with God's promise.

Review these seven moves and the circumstances surrounding them as often as necessary until the **sequence AND the circumstances surrounding each move** is clearly lodged in your mind. **Once you know the**

sequence and the circumstances, you will be able in total darkness to go through the Old Testament in skeleton form from beginning to end.

Assignment For This Chapter

1. Fill in the blanks on the map on the next page.

2. Mentally picture the location of the following places:
   (1) The Persian Gulf; (2) Egypt; (3) The Fertile Crescent; (4) The Mediterranean Sea; (5) Israel; (6) Ur; (7) Eden; (8) Babylon; (9) Haran.

3. Name the seven major moves.

   Move #1: from ____________________ to ____________________

   Move #2: from ____________________ to ____________________

   Move #3: from ____________________ to ____________________

   Move #4: from ____________________ to ____________________

   Move #5: from ____________________ to ____________________

   Move #6: from ____________________ to ____________________

   Move #7: from ____________________ to ____________________

4. Trace all seven moves on the map on the next page.

5. Briefly describe the circumstances surrounding each move, why it was made, and how it fits into God's overall plan.

   Move #1: FROM EDEN TO UR: ____________________

   ____

   ____

   ____

   ____

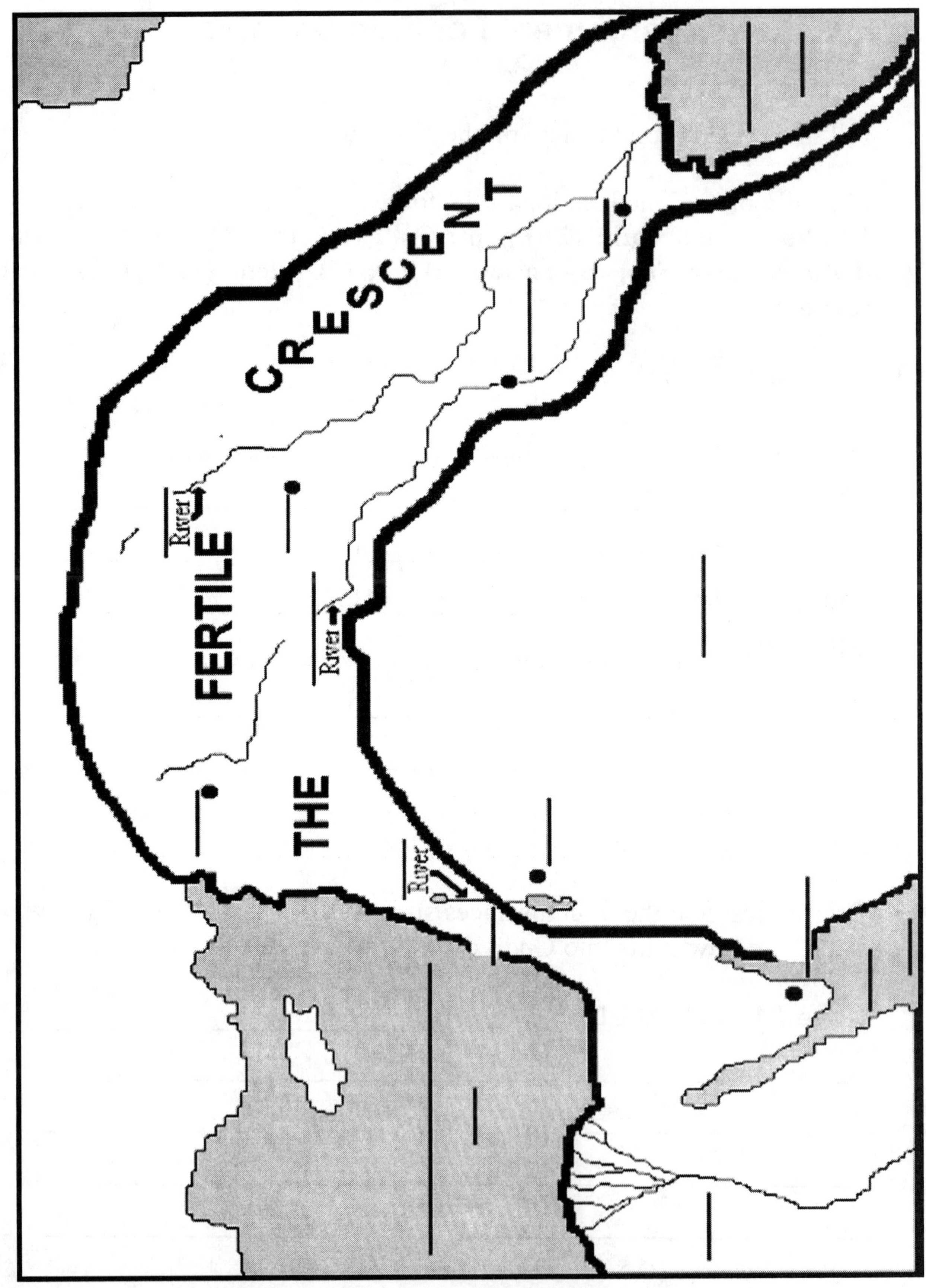
THE
FERTILE
CRESCENT
River
River
River

Move #2: FROM UR TO HARAN: ______________________________

____

____

____

____

____

Move #3: FROM HARAN TO ISRAEL: ________________________

____

____

____

____

____

Move #4: FROM ISRAEL TO EGYPT: ________________________

____

____

____

____

____

Move #5: FROM EGYPT BACK TO ISRAEL: _______________

____

____

____

____

____

Move #6: FROM ISRAEL TO BABYLON: ________________

____

____

____

____

____

Move #7: FROM BABYLON BACK TO ISRAEL: ___________

____

____

____

____

____

6. Read the story of all seven major moves **directly from scripture.** (See page 137.)

Eight Quick And Easy Ways To Get A Clear-Focused Overview Of The Entire Old Testament

STEP NUMBER 2:

THE TWENTY KEY PEOPLE OF THE OLD TESTAMENT

THE TWENTY KEY PEOPLE (or GROUPS of people)

Another excellent way to get a good, clear, mental picture of the Old Testament is to become acquainted with several of the key people **and remember them in sequence**.

Beginning with Adam, I have chosen 20 key people (or GROUPS of people) that form a chain throughout the entire Old Testament.

Someone has said that there are 2,930 people named in the Bible -- the most of which are in the Old Testament. **But every single one** of the hundreds and hundreds of people named in the Old Testament can in **one way or another be connected** with one or more of the twenty people that have been chosen.

I suggest that you think of these twenty key people as "twenty links" in a chain. Examine each one to be sure that you understand exactly who they are, what they did, and how they fit into God's overall plan. Then after becoming very comfortable with your knowledge of these twenty people and their place in God's plan, **simply connect each one to the person before them and the person after them, and you have a chain that goes through the entire Old Testament.**

It's that simple -- knowing and understanding only twenty people -- and you have the entire Old Testament fitly framed together.

Another exciting thing is that not only will you have the complete framework clearly in your mind, but you will now have **twenty solid "posts" scattered throughout the entire Old Testament** with which to **associate every single** Old Testament event that you ever read about or hear of **for the rest of your life**.

Now, let's examine these key people and begin to "link" them together.

THE SIX IN GENESIS

The story of six of them is found in the book of Genesis. This is almost one-third of the twenty in only one book, but it will not seem unusual to have one-third of them in one book when you consider the fact that **the Book of Genesis covers a longer period of time than all the rest of the Old Testament and the New Testament combined. In fact, just the first eleven chapters alone cover 2,100 years -- over half of the 4,000 years of the Old Testament!** This is important to remember -- the story of over half of the Old Testament period in only the first eleven chapters!

There are two key people during this 2,100 years -- **Adam**, the father of the human race, and **Noah**, through whom the world was spared and repopulated.

At the end of these first eleven chapters, we come to the **very pivot point** of the entire Bible. **The first three verses of chapter 12 are what John Stott refers to as "perhaps the most unifying verses of the whole Bible," because they set the stage for everything** that will happen **from here through Revelation**. In these three verses, God makes two promises to **Abraham**. In verse two, He promises to make a great nation out of Abraham and then makes an even greater promise in verse three when He tells Abraham that all families of the earth will be blessed through him.

Here is what Stott calls "the plot for the entire Bible." From this point on, **the entire balance of the Old Testament is the story** of the nation that God promised to make of Abraham and God's dealings with that nation. ***And* the promise that "all families of the earth (would be) blessed" through Abraham's seed is the story of the New Testament**.

With this thought in mind, it will now be easy to "link" the remaining key people together and see how they fit into God's overall plan for the ages.

From this point on, we see that ***nation*** slowly come into existence -- first of all, of course, as a ***family***. Abraham has a son named **Isaac** who then has a son. Isaac's son was originally named **Jacob**, but God changed his name to Israel (the name by which this promised nation will later be called).

Jacob, or Israel as his name was changed to, then has twelve sons. I will not list the names of all twelve of them here, but in order to tie the key people together, I will mention only his son **Joseph**.

As years passed, each of Jacob's children had families of their own which kept multiplying until each of these large families is referred to as a **"Tribe."** This, of course, is where we get the phrase **"The Twelve Tribes of Israel."** And since the entire nation descended from Jacob/Israel, the nation is often referred to as "The children of Israel." They literally were Israel's "children" or descendants.

The story of these six key people from the book of Genesis -- Adam, Noah, Abraham, Isaac, Jacob, and Joseph -- covers the entire period of time from creation until the nation that God promised to make of Abraham had come into existence. Abraham's ***Family*** has now become the ***Nation*** of Israel.

Review the chart on the following page and be sure that all six are fixed firmly and in proper sequence in your mind.

THE SIX IN GENESIS

ADAM

NOAH

ABRAHAM

ISAAC

JACOB

JOSEPH

ISRAEL'S ELEVEN LEADERS

From Exodus on, the entire balance of the Old Testament is the story of the nation of Israel and of God's dealings with it. You could, of course, say that the story of Israel begins in the twelfth chapter of Genesis when God made the promise to Abraham; and you would be correct. However, I prefer to use Exodus as the point to begin referring to them as a **nation rather than just a family,** because one of the very first verses of Exodus (Ex. 1:7) states, "And the children of Israel (Jacob) were fruitful, and increased abundantly, and multiplied, and waxed exceeding mighty; and the land was filled with them."

Another reason that I choose Exodus as the point to begin referring to them as a nation is the fact that prior to this time in Egypt, there had been no leader chosen or appointed to lead them as one body. There had, of course, been the Patriarchs who had authority over and led their own individual families; but there had been no special appointed leader to lead and guide the entire nation. But early in Exodus -- in chapters two and three -- God raised up Moses to be the very first leader of what had then become a very large body of people.

So, to the six key people in Genesis I have added **Israel's eleven leaders**. You see, if you "group" the twelve Judges together as one and then also "group" the 39 kings of the divided kingdom together as one, **Israel only had eleven leaders (or GROUPS of leaders)** during the entire Old Testament period. Again, **it is absolutely amazing how clear-focused the entire Old Testament** becomes simply by knowing these eleven leaders **in sequence, what was going on in their lifetime, and the "flow" of what God was doing in their generations!**

For a complete listing of these leaders, look at the chart on the following page.

ISRAEL'S ELEVEN LEADERS (or GROUPS of Leaders)

1. MOSES
2. JOSHUA
3. THE TWELVE JUDGES
4. SAMUEL
5. SAUL
6. DAVID
7. SOLOMON
8. THE 39 KINGS OF THE DIVIDED KINGDOM
9. ZERUBBABEL
10. EZRA
11. NEHEMIAH

Now, in order to "link" them together in an easily understood and easily remembered chain, let's take them one by one and examine them more closely.

1. Moses. When Jacob's *FAMILY* moved into Egypt, the "population" of this "great nation" that God had promised to make of Abraham was only 70. But they very quickly multiplied, and the population grew to more than two million while in Egypt.

For generations as this nation was developing, they had no **definite leader.** However, after they began to be so cruelly treated by the Egyptians, God appeared to Moses at the "burning bush" and commissioned him as Israel's very first leader.

In obedience to God, Moses went to Pharaoh and demanded that God's people be allowed to go free. When Pharaoh resisted, God worked mighty miracles through Moses. God sent ten grievous plagues to "convince" Pharaoh. Moses then led them in a mass exodus from Egypt and for the next 40 years, proved to be one of Israel's greatest leaders. In fact, his leadership was so significant that the story of Moses covers **more than one-seventh** of the entire Bible.

2. Joshua. Israel's second leader was Joshua. During the wilderness wanderings, God had been grooming Joshua. Shortly after Moses' death, God spoke to Joshua and commissioned him to lead the children of Israel on into the Promised Land. Under his leadership, they miraculously crossed the Jordan River, conquered the land, and divided it among the twelve tribes. For the rest of his life, Joshua led them through this important "conquest period."

3. The 12 Judges. After the death of Joshua, there was a 400-year period when "there was no king" in the land and "every man did that which was right in his own eyes." During that 400 years, Israel repeatedly went through the 5-step cycle shown on the next page and on the chart following.

Step 1: They would stray from God.

Step 2: God would allow a neighboring country to overrun them.

Step 3: They would cry out to God for deliverance.

Step 4: God would raise up a deliverer (Judge).

Step 5: They would faithfully serve God for a period of time before beginning the 5-step cycle all over again.

THE TIME OF THE JUDGES

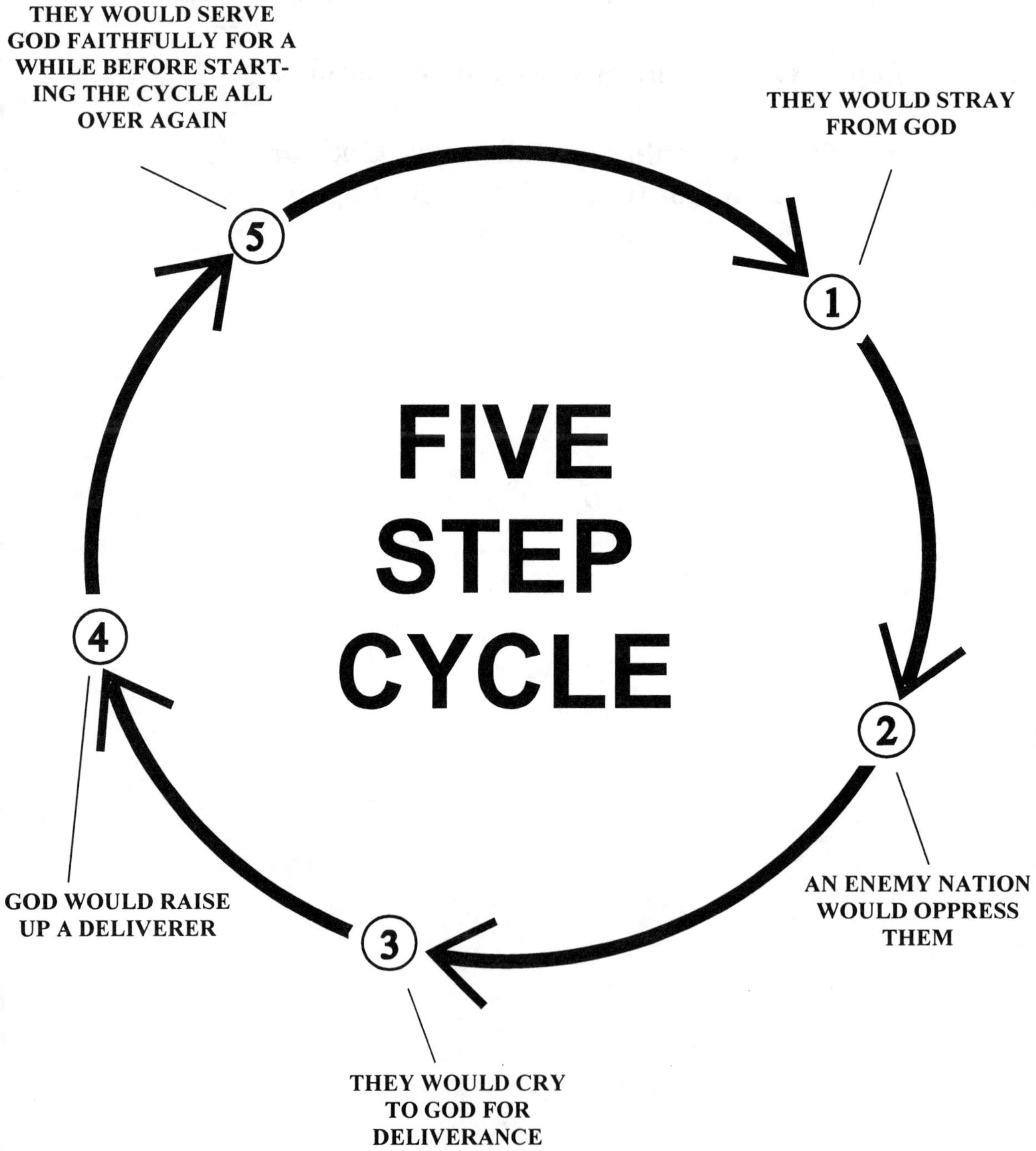

FIVE STEP CYCLE

1. THEY WOULD STRAY FROM GOD
2. AN ENEMY NATION WOULD OPPRESS THEM
3. THEY WOULD CRY TO GOD FOR DELIVERANCE
4. GOD WOULD RAISE UP A DELIVERER
5. THEY WOULD SERVE GOD FAITHFULLY FOR A WHILE BEFORE STARTING THE CYCLE ALL OVER AGAIN

Seven times during that 400 year period they went through this **5-step cycle,** and each time God raised up one or more Judges to deliver them.

There are a number of things that we need to learn from this period. Over and over, God made it abundantly clear that **sin and disobedience will ALWAYS be judged** and that **righteousness and obedience will ALWAYS be rewarded.** His judgment and rewards are not always immediate, **but with absolute certainty they will come.**

The Bible says, **"because sentence** against an evil work **is not executed speedily,** . . . the heart . . . is fully set . . . to do evil." (Ecc. 8:11). It further states, "though a sinner do evil an hundred times, and **his days be prolonged,** yet surely I know that **it shall be well with them that fear God . . .** ***but it shall not be well*** **with the wicked."** (vv. 12-13).

Our own lifetime may not be long enough to see the absolute certainty of God's rewards and His judgment; because, indeed, "sentence against an evil work" is not always "executed speedily;" and rewards do not always come immediately. However, one of the tremendous benefits that we receive from studying the Old Testament is that it allows us to see a far bigger time frame than our own lifetime. Our lifetime may not always show it; **but when the centuries are all blended together,** one fact becomes clear:

> **God will see to it that righteousness and obedience will** *always* **be put on the throne and that sin, wickedness, and disobedience will** *always* **be put to the scaffold.**

In the entire 4,000 ye ars of the Old Testament **not one single person** failed to be judged for his or her sins; and **not one single person** failed to be rewarded for obedience and righteousness. And we can be sure that this law of God still applies to us today!

4. Samuel. Although Samuel was one of the Judges, we list him separately because he was more than a Judge. He was a prophet, a seer, and was one of Israel's most colorful leaders. It was during his lifetime that the transition was made from ***tribal government*** to Israel's being led by a ***king***. Unwilling for Samuel's sons to lead them, Israel's elders came to Samuel and demanded a ***king***. This greatly displeased Samuel; but when he carried their demand before the Lord, Samuel was instructed to go ahead and "make them a king." He obeyed and anointed the first ***king*** over the nation of Israel.

5. Saul. The man that Samuel anointed was Saul. After the transition from tribal government, there were only three men who served over the entire nation of Israel before it was divided and became **two** nations. Saul was the first of these three men. However, Saul disobeyed and greatly displeased the Lord. Because of this disobedience, God rejected him and had Samuel anoint a young lad to take Saul's place.

6. David. The young lad that God chose to take Saul's place was David. God now further reveals that it is going to be **through David's family** that the promise to Abraham will be fulfilled. God made a covenant with David and promised him that when "thou shalt sleep with thy fathers, I will set up thy seed after thee . . . and thine house and thy kingdom shall be established for ever."

Through David, God begins a **family line of kings** that continued throughout the entire Old Testament period and then had its **true fulfillment** in the birth of Christ who was born of the lineage of David (and, of course, the lineage of Abraham as well). It was Christ who was the **"real"** seed that God had spoken of to Abraham and to David. It was He who would be the **"eternal king"** that God spoke of to David and **"the seed"** that He spoke about to Abraham.

7. Solomon. After David's death, God's promise to David that his "house and . . . kingdom (would) be established for ever" had its **first step of fulfillment** when his son, Solomon, became king. Although Solomon was the final king to serve over the entire nation with all twelve tribes still joined together, this **family line of kings** continued on as we will see when we look at the next GROUP of leaders.

8. The 39 Kings of the Divided Kingdom. Shortly after Solomon's death when his son, Rehoboam, would have been king over the nation of Israel, a very important event took place. The people came to Rehoboam and said, "thy father (Solomon) made our yoke grievous." The people asked Rehoboam to "lighten their burdens." He refused their request and in refusing said to them, "my father did lade you with a heavy yoke, I will add to your yoke: my father . . . chastised you will whips, . . . I will chastise you with scorpions." In rebellion to this response, ten of the tribes separated themselves and **set up a new kingdom.** From that time onward, **there were two nations.**

Since the northern kingdom with ten tribes was far larger than the two tribes that remained in the southern kingdom, they kept the name Israel and just simply selected a king and established themselves in a new capital city.

Only two tribes -- Judah and Benjamin -- remained with Rehoboam. Since Judah was much larger than the small tribe of Benjamin, the whole nation began to be called by the name Judah. Jerusalem continued to be their capital, and Rehoboam was established as the first king of the nation of Judah.

It is extremely important to remember that although it was much smaller than the 10-tribe nation to the north, Judah was by far the most important. It is Judah where David's "seed" would continue the **family line of kings** that God promised; **and it is from the nation (and tribe) of Judah that Christ was born**. You will recall that in Revelation Jesus is referred to as "the lion of the tribe of Judah".

For a comparison of the two nations, see the chart on the following page.

A COMPARISON OF THE TWO NATIONS

NORTH -- SOUTH

ISRAEL -- JUDAH

10 TRIBES -- 2 TRIBES

SAMARIA -- JERUSALEM

19 KINGS -- 20 KINGS

NO GOOD KINGS -- 8 GOOD KINGS

The next two to three hundred years of the divided kingdom were marked with serious straying from God. Repeatedly, the prophets warned that unless Israel turned back to God they would be destroyed; but they paid God's messengers very little heed. In fact, of the 19 kings who reigned over the northern kingdom of Israel, **not one of them** ever attempted to bring the people back to God.

In the southern kingdom of Judah, there were at least a few times of revival. Of the 20 kings who reigned there, eight sought to follow God; and the nation at least at times experienced some measure of revival. However, on the whole, they too strayed from God.

As a direct result of their disobedience, God allowed both nations to go into exile. The ten tribes of the northern kingdom of Israel were "scattered" by the Assyrians. We sometimes speak of the "ten lost tribes of Israel," because they never returned as a nation.

Having experienced at least some measure of occasional revival, the southern kingdom of Judah continued for 100 years or so after Israel was destroyed. But after repeated refusal to heed God's message, they too went into captivity when God allowed Nebuchadnezzar to come and carry them captive to Babylon.

9. Zerubbabel. After 70 years of captivity in Babylon, God restored Judah to their homeland. God raised up three men who led three different groups back to Jerusalem. The first of these three was Zerubbabel.

10. Ezra. The second return to Jerusalem was led by Ezra.

11. Nehemiah. The third and final return was led by Nehemiah.

THE OTHER THREE . . . .

We have already looked at seventeen of the twenty key people -- the six in Genesis and Israel's eleven leaders. That leaves three more to complete the twenty. For two of that remaining three, two of Israel's arch enemies -- **Pharaoh and Nebuchadnezzar** -- have been chosen.

These two men are mentioned in scripture several dozen times each and figure very prominently in the history and message of the Old Testament.

Then, for the final one of the twenty, **all of the prophets** have been grouped together and listed as one. These are the men that God raised up and sent to warn Israel when they strayed, urging them to follow in close step with God. The prophets are the ones **who truly thread together the real message and the history of the Old Testament**, and certainly no listing of key people would be complete without them.

THE OTHER THREE

Pharaoh

Nebuchadnezzar

The Prophets

The chart on the following page reviews all twenty and places them into the following groups.

1. The Six in Genesis.
2. Israel's Eleven Leaders (or Groups of leaders).
3. The Other Three.

Be sure to become familiar with all twenty of them and see the “flow” of how each one fits into God’s overall plan for the ages. Then by linking them together as a chain you can see in skeleton form the entire Old Testament. Once again, with nothing but these 20 people **in sequence** and an understanding of who they are, what they did, and how they fit into God’s overall plan, **you can in total darkness go through the entire Old Testament in skeleton form.**

THE 20 KEY PEOPLE OF THE OLD TESTAMENT

THE SIX IN GENESIS

ADAM
NOAH
ABRAHAM
ISAAC
JACOB
JOSEPH

ISRAEL'S ELEVEN LEADERS

MOSES
JOSHUA
THE TWELVE JUDGES
SAMUEL
SAUL
DAVID
SOLOMON
THE 39 KINGS OF THE DIVIDED KINGDOM
ZERUBBABEL
EZRA
NEHEMIAH

THE OTHER THREE

PHARAOH
NEBUCHADNEZZAR
THE PROPHETS

Assignment For This Chapter

1. Name the twenty key people of the Old Testament.

The Six in Genesis

1. ______________________________
2. ______________________________
3. ______________________________
4. ______________________________
5. ______________________________
6. ______________________________

Israel's Eleven Leaders

1. ______________________________
2. ______________________________
3. ______________________________
4. ______________________________
5. ______________________________
6. ______________________________
7. ______________________________
8. ______________________________
9. ______________________________
10. ______________________________
11. ______________________________

The Other Three

1. ______________________________
2. ______________________________
3. ______________________________

2. Give a brief description of each of the twenty key people (use additional paper if needed)

The Six in Genesis

Adam: ____________________

____

____

____

Noah: ____________________

____

____

____

Abraham: ____________________

____

____

____

Isaac: ____________________

____

____

____

Jacob: ____________________

____

____

____

Joseph: ____________________

____

____

____

Israel's Eleven Leaders (or Groups of Leaders)

Moses:

Joshua:

The Twelve Judges:

Samuel:

Saul:

David:

Solomon:

The Thirty-Nine Kings of the Divided Kingdom:____________

Zerubbabel:____________

Ezra:____________

Nehemiah:____________

The Other Three

Pharoah:____________

Nebuchadnezzar:____________

The Prophets:____

____

____

____

3. Read the story of the twenty key people directly from scripture. (See page 137-138.)

4. Explain the significance of Genesis 12:1-3 and the two promises that God made to Abraham in those three verses. (Use a separate sheet of paper.)

5. Identify the "Five-Step Cycle" that Israel repeatedly went through during the 400-year period of the Judges.

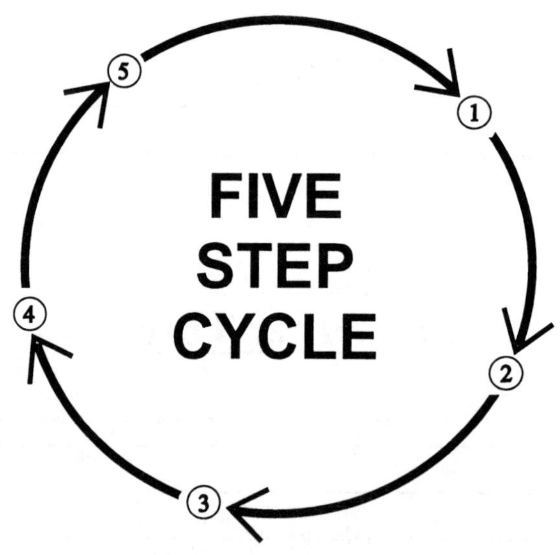

1. ____
2. ____
3. ____
4. ____
5. ____

6. Fill in the blanks below to give a comparison of the two nations that formed when the 12 tribes were split apart.

THE NATION IN THE NORTH		THE NATION IN THE SOUTH
___________	NAME	___________
___________	NUMBER OF TRIBES	___________
___________	CAPITAL	___________
___________	NUMBER OF KINGS	___________
___ GOOD KINGS	← →	___ GOOD KINGS

Eight Quick And Easy Ways To Get A Clear-Focused Overview Of The Entire Old Testament

STEP NUMBER 3:

THE THREE MAJOR DIVISIONS OF THE OLD TESTAMENT

THE THREE MAJOR DIVISIONS OF THE OLD TESTAMENT

The Bible is not only the most marvelous Book in the whole world; it is also the most "marvelously written."
As for content, no other book even comes close. It contains **God's message to mankind**, and nothing else could even remotely be as important as that.

Nor does any other book come close when you consider the style and method in which it was written. The Bible was written **over a 1500 year period of time** by approximately 40 divinely inspired writers who wrote "as they were moved by the Holy Ghost" (2 Peter 1:21). These men not only came from "different generations," but they also came from different occupations and backgrounds. There were kings, princes, priests, prophets, farm laborers, herdsmen, physicians, lawyers, teachers, tax collectors, and fishermen. Approximately 30 of them were writers of the Old Testament (those **before** the time of Christ), and the rest wrote the books of the New Testament (those written **after** the time of Christ).

For centuries these inspired writings remained in separate scrolls with no attempt to combine them in a single book. Gradually, a few of them began to be grouped together; and by the time of Christ the Old Testament scriptures fell into **three** divisions, all three of which were referred to by Jesus in the New Testament. Notice the chart on the next page to see these groupings.

THE THREE GROUPINGS REFERRED TO IN THE NEW TESTAMENT

1. **The Law of Moses** (or simply **the Law**). This was made up of the first five books that we now call **the Pentateuch** (Genesis through Deuteronomy).

2. **The Prophets**. This division was further divided into the **"Former Prophets"** and the **"Latter Prophets."** The **"Former Prophets"** contained Joshua, Judges, 1 & 2 Samuel, and 1 & 2 Kings **which provided the continuous narrative of Israel from the crossing of Jordan to the exile in Babylon.** The **"Latter Prophets"** contained Isaiah, Jeremiah, and the twelve minor prophets.

3. **The Writings** (sometimes called **the Psalms**). This group contained the balance of the books not included in the two divisions above. The reason they were sometimes called **the Psalms** was due to the fact that the **book** of Psalms **was the first** of the books in this group and is larger than any of the others.

As long as each book was in a separate scroll, **sequence** had not mattered. However, after the invention of the printing press, it was quickly decided to combine all of the Holy Scriptures in one book. Now, a clear-cut decision had to be made as to sequence -- which book would follow which, etc. To a large degree, the groupings remained somewhat similar to the three groups you have just reviewed. The major differences were:

1. The **"Former** Prophets" and six of the books from "The Writings" were combined with **"The Law."** This was done because all seventeen of these books are **"historical"** in nature. These are the ones that give **the story** of the entire Old Testament period, so they are called the **Historical Books.** The decision was then made to place them at the **very beginning** of the Old Testament.

2. After the "historical" books had been combined, all of the books that are **"prophetical"** in nature were then grouped together. The decision was made to just place them **as a group** at the **very end** of the Old Testament rather than attempt to "interweave" them among the other books.

3. After all of the books that were "historical" in nature and all of the "prophetical" books had been separated, there were five books remaining. **Since all five of these were originally written as Hebrew poetry,** they are known as the **Poetical Books**. As for sequence, this group of five was placed between the 17 Historical Books and the 17 Prophetical Books.

Officially, these three groups are known as **the Historical Books, the Poetical Books,** and **the Prophetical Books;** but for simplicity, I call them the **STORY**, the **SONGS**, and the **SERMONS** of the Old Testament. To stamp this is your mind, I suggest that you turn to the table of contents in your own Bible and draw a small line after the book of Esther and another small line after the book of Song of Solomon. At the side of the first group, write **STORY**; at the side of the last group, write **SERMONS**; and at the side of the middle group, write **SONGS.**

INTERESTING FACTS AND SIMILARITIES

There are some very interesting facts and similarities about these three groupings that can be very useful in helping you “locate” and “identify” each of these books in your mind.

For instance:

INTERESTING FACTS AND SIMILARITIES

There are **Seventeen** Historical Books
AND
There are **Seventeen** Prophetical Books
17 - 17

The **Historical Books** are the **VERY FIRST 17** books of the Old Testament
AND
The **Prophetical Books** are the **VERY LAST 17** books of the Old Testament

---

The **Poetical Books** are then **squarely in the middle** of these **two groups of 17**

HISTORICAL	POETICAL	PROPHETICAL
Genesis	Job	Isaiah
Exodus	Psalms	Jeremiah
Leviticus	Proverbs	Lamentations
Numbers	Ecclesiastes	Ezekiel
Deuteronomy	Song of Solomon	Daniel
Joshua		Hosea
Judges		Joel
Ruth		Amos
I Samuel		Obadiah
II Samuel		Jonah
I Kings		Micah
II Kings		Nahum
I Chronicles		Habakkuk
II Chronicles		Zephaniah
Ezra		Haggai
Nehemiah		Zechariah
Esther		Malachi

INTERESTING FACTS AND SIMILARITIES (CONTINUED)

The 17 Historical Books are further
divided into two groups of 5 and 12

AND

The 17 Prophetical Books are **further divided into two groups of 5 and 12**

Historical 5 - 12 - 17 **Prophetical 5 - 12 - 17**

The 17 Historical books are divided into the **Pentateuch (5 books)** and the **other Historical Books (12)**

5 - 12 - 17

AND

The 17 Prophetical Books are divided into the **Major Prophets (5)** and the **Minor Prophets (12)**

5 - 12 - 17

There are **5** Books in the **Pentateuch**
There are **5 Poetical Books**
There are **5 Major Prophets**

5 - 5 - 5

There are **12 other Historical Books**
There are **12 Minor Prophets**

12 - 12

Assignment For This Chapter

1. The three major divisions of the Old Testament are the _________ books, the __________ books, and the _________ books.

2. Another name for the three groups could be the ____________, the __________, and the __________ of the Old Testament.

3. The **first 17 books** of the Old Testament are the _________ books.

4. The **last 17 books** of the Old Testament are the _________ books.

5. The _________ books are squarely in the middle of the 17 Historical books and the 17 Prophetical books.

6. The first five Historical books are called _____ __________.

7. The first five Prophetical books are _____ _____ ________.

8. There are ____ Historical books and there are ____ Prophetical books.

9. There are ___ books in the Pentateuch, ___ Poetical books, and ___ Major Prophets.

10. In addition to the Pentateuch, there are ____ ***other*** Historical books; and there are ____ Minor Prophets.

11. Name the thirty-nine books of the Old Testament by filling in the spaces below.

HISTORICAL BOOKS

The Pentateuch

____
____
____
____
____

Other Historical

____
____
____
____
____
____
____
____
____
____
____
____

POETICAL BOOKS

____
____
____
____
____

PROPHETICAL BOOKS

Major Prophets

____
____
____
____
____

Minor Prophets

____
____
____
____
____
____
____
____
____
____
____
____

Eight Quick And Easy Ways To Get A Clear-Focused Overview Of The Entire Old Testament

STEP NUMBER 4:

THE ELEVEN BOOKS THAT CONTAIN MORE THAN 95% OF THE NARRATIVE OF THE OLD TESTAMENT

THE ELEVEN BOOKS THAT CONTAIN MORE THAN 95% OF THE NARRATIVE OF THE OLD TESTAMENT

It comes as quite a surprise to many people to learn that **more than 95% of the narrative, or story, of the Old Testament is contained in only eleven books.** Many people think of the Old Testament as just "skipping about;" but if you take these eleven by themselves, it gives a **continuous, uninterrupted story just as continuous as a book that you will get off the shelf of any library or bookstore.**

By looking at these as a unit, you can easily see **the continuity of the story.** That is very important because **by seeing it in a continuous manner, it will be far easier to understand AND far easier to remember.** (The chart on the next page gives a listing of the eleven).

THE ELEVEN BOOKS THAT CONTAIN MORE THAN 95% OF THE NARRATIVE OF THE OLD TESTAMENT

* Genesis
* Exodus
* Numbers
* Joshua
* Judges
* I & II Samuel
* I & II Kings
* Ezra
* Nehemiah

It is very important to realize that at the end of Nehemiah, the *story* of the Old Testament is already complete.

If you have never read the entire Old Testament, I would strongly suggest that you begin by reading these eleven books first. This will establish **the narrative** completely in your mind. After you have a good understanding of the **STORY,** you will then find that the other 28 books fit in place much easier and clearer.

The remaining 28 books fall into three categories. Take time to review the chart on the following page to get acquainted with them. This will give you a good grasp of the "setting" for each book. Also, be sure to examine the other charts in this section. Each one is designed to further establish the **story of the Old Testament** firmly in your mind and to help you "locate" and "identify" each of the books, thus making it easier for you to "travel through" the Old Testament without any "bumps."

THE REMAINING 28 BOOKS

1. **THE OTHER SIX HISTORICAL BOOKS.** In addition to the eleven already mentioned, there are **six other H i s torical books -- Deuteronomy, I & II Chronicles, Ruth, Esther, and Leviticus.** The first three are primarily **summary books** and **enlargements** on the events covered in one or more previous books. Ruth and Esther contain the beautiful stories of those two great women, and Leviticus gives detailed instructions for Israel's ceremonial and religious life. (The chart on the following page shows these six sequenced in with the eleven).

2. **THE FIVE POETICAL BOOKS** of Job, Psalms, Proverbs, Ecclesiastes, and Song of Solomon were all originally written as Hebrew poetry. They deal with many extremely important spiritual truths and issues of every day life.

3. **THE PROPHETICAL BOOKS** contain the messages of the Prophets that God sent to warn Israel, Judah, and surrounding nations to turn from their sins and faithfully live for Him. **Every single one of these fit into the events and the time period covered in 1 & 2 Kings, Ezra, and Nehemiah.** Instead of "splicing" each Prophet's message chronologically among the historical books, all seventeen were grouped together and placed at the end of the Old Testament.

THE 17 HISTORICAL BOOKS

THE ELEVEN WHICH CONTAIN 95% OF THE STORY	THE OTHER SIX
* GENESIS	
* EXODUS	
	* LEVITICUS
* NUMBERS	
	* DEUTERONOMY
* JOSHUA	
* JUDGES	
	* RUTH
* I & II SAMUEL	
* I & II KINGS	
	* I & II CHRONICLES
* EZRA	
* NEHEMIAH	
	* ESTHER

HIGHLIGHTS OF THE NARRATIVE BOOKS AND THE PORTION OF THE OLD TESTAMENT STORY CONTAINED IN EACH

GENESIS: Creation to the death of Joseph in Egypt.

EXODUS: The birth of Moses until the setting up of the Tabernacle at Mt. Sinai.

NUMBERS: The wilderness journey from Mt. Sinai until arrival at the edge of the Promised Land and preparation to enter.

JOSHUA: The entrance and conquest of Canaan until the death of Joshua.

JUDGES: The 400-year period of the Judges.

I SAMUEL: The birth of Samuel and the reign of Israel's FIRST king -- King Saul.

II SAMUEL: The reign of David.

I KINGS: The reign of Solomon, the breaking away of 10 of the 12 Tribes to form a separate NATION, and the reign of the first few kings of the Divided Kingdom. (First Kings also contains the story of the Prophet ELIJAH).

II KINGS: The reign of the remaining kings of the Divided Kingdom until Israel is "scattered" by the Assyrians and Judah is carried captive to Babylon. (Second Kings also contains the story of the prophet ELISHA).

EZRA: The return from Babylonian Exile until the Temple is rebuilt.

NEHEMIAH: The final phase of the return from Exile and the rebuilding of the walls of Jerusalem.

Assignment For This Chapter

1. Name the eleven books that contain more than 95% of the narrative of the Old Testament. (Use separate sheet.)

2. Give the portion of the Old Testament narrative found in each of those eleven books.

Genesis:____

Exodus:____

Numbers:____

Joshua:____

Judges:____

1 Samuel:____

2 Samuel:____

1 Kings:____

2 Kings:____

Ezra:____

Nehemiah: ____

Eight Quick And Easy Ways To Get A Clear-Focused Overview Of The Entire Old Testament

STEP NUMBER 5:

An Easy Way To Remember The Basic Contents Of Each Of The Books Of The Old Testament

AN EASY WAY TO REMEMBER THE BASIC CONTENTS OF EACH OF THE BOOKS OF THE OLD TESTAMENT

The charts on the following pages give you an easy way to remember the basic contents of each of the Old Testament books. They are listed in four groupings:

1. **The Eleven Books that CONTAIN MORE THAN 95% OF THE STORY of the Old Testament.**

2. **THE OTHER SIX HISTORICAL BOOKS.**

3. **THE POETICAL BOOKS.**

4. **THE PROPHETICAL BOOKS.**

I have sought for things that will kind of "latch on to you" and will be easy to remember. Be sure to review these charts frequently until you have a good mental picture of the basic contents of each book. Having a general idea of the contents of each book will **greatly** help you to locate specific verses and events that you will have need to search for from time to time throughout the rest of your life.

GENESIS

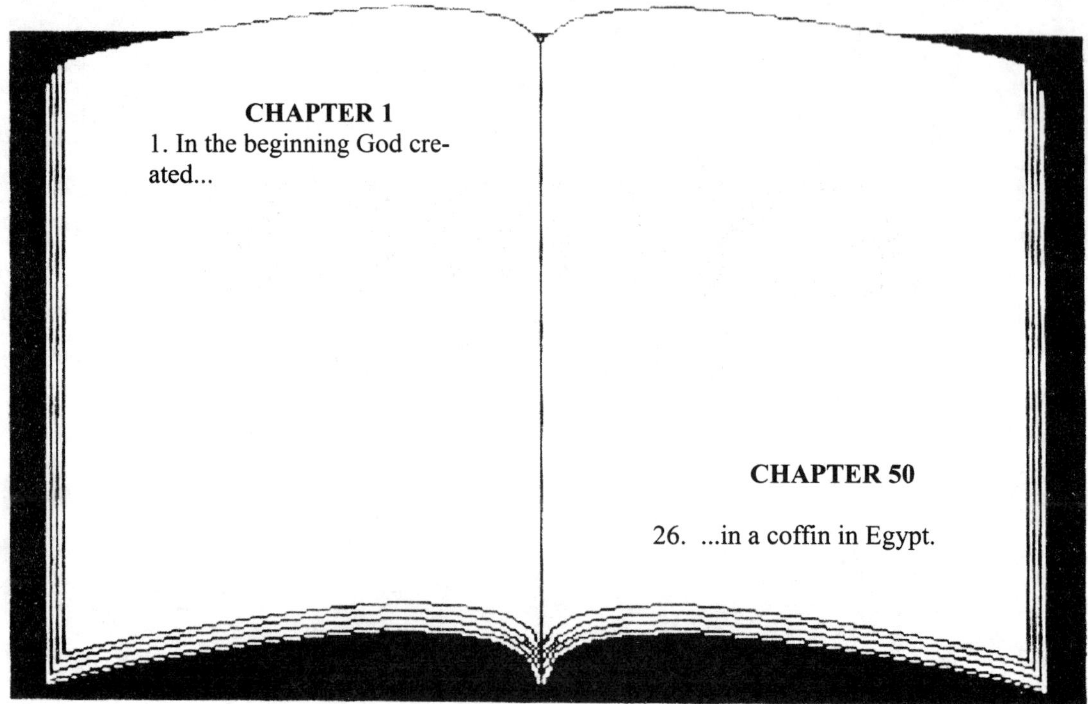

The two very best ways that I know of to remember the basic contents of Genesis is first of all to simply be aware that **IT COVERS THE ENTIRE PERIOD BEFORE ISRAEL BECAME A NATION;** and the second way is to remember **the first five words** and **the last five words.** Almost everyone already knows that the first five words are "In the beginning God created..." but many do not know that the **last** five words are **"...in a coffin in Egypt."** These are the boundaries -- everything from **creation** to **Joseph's death and being placed in a coffin in Egypt** is found in Genesis.

EXODUS

(Mass Departure -- Exit)

The very best way to remember the basic contents of Exodus is simply by the definition **-- a mass departure -- EXIT**. And that's what you have in Exodus -- the Exodus from Egypt along with the circumstances leading up to it and the events that took place immediately thereafter.

The book of Numbers gets its name from the two **Censuses** it contains, **or as it was called at that time "NUMBERings."** The first was shortly after the Israelites left Egypt, and the second was almost 40 years later just before they entered The Promised Land. **Numbers contains those two Censuses and the 40 years in between which were the years of wilderness wanderings.**

THE BALANCE OF THE NARRATIVE BOOKS

BOOK	LEADER
JOSHUA	JOSHUA
JUDGES	THE 12 JUDGES
I SAMUEL	SAMUEL & SAUL
II SAMUEL	DAVID
I KINGS	SOLOMON*
II KINGS	THE 39 KINGS OF THE DIVIDED KINGDOM
EZRA	ZERUBBABEL & EZRA
NEHEMIAH	NEHEMIAH

The very best way to remember the basic contents of the balance of the narrative books is by **remembering whose story is found in that book.** In the 8 books listed above, the story of all Israel's leaders **after Moses** is found. Since there are 8 books and 10 leaders, there are two books which have more that one leader's story. **Other than that you can go down the list and assign one book to each leader;** and that will be the basic content of that book -- the story and circumstances of the leadership, life, and time period of that particular leader (or GROUP of leaders).

NOTE: You will find some of the leaders **mentioned** in the books **preceding** their book while God was **"grooming"** them for leadership; **but the story of their administration** -- the time they were leader -- is found in the books shown above.

***The only exception is the fact that when the story of Solomon's reign is completed the story goes immediately to the dividing of the kingdom and the first few king's story** is included; **but the story of the majority of the kings of the divided kingdom** is found in the book of Second Kings shown above.

THE THREE "SUMMARY" BOOKS

DEUTERonomy

The prefix DEUTER or DEUTERO means "second in a series." Deuteronomy is the "second in a series" in two ways. The Law which had been given approximately 40 years before is now taught to the "new generation" ant it **summarizes** the account of the Wilderness Wanderings.

I CHRONICLES

II CHRONICLES

These two books **summarize** the Kingdom Period which has already been covered in First & Second Samuel and First and Second Kings. First Chronicles **summarizes David's kingship.** Second Chronicles **summarizes** that of Solomon and the period of the Divided Kingdom. However, one major difference is that once the kingdom is divided into the two nations of Judah and Israel, **Second Chronicles only covers** the history of **Judah** (the nation from which Christ came), whereas Samuel and Kings cover the history of both Israel and Judah.

THE TWO BIOGRAPHIES

RUTH

"WHITHER THOU GOEST, I WILL GO."

ESTHER

"IF I PERISH, I PERISH."

A good way to remember the contents of Ruth and Esther is to simply be aware of the fact that rather than advancing the general theme of the Old Testament these two books are biographies of the two great women that the books are named for. Then by remembering the well-known quotation that each one made, you can call to mind the story of their life which is the theme of these two books.

Leviticus could be referred to as the "Priest's Handbook." **Exodus ended with the Tabernacle being set up for the very first time.** Now that the Tabernacle is set up, the priests (and the people) must know God's plan for worship. God gave Moses detailed instructions for Tabernacle worship, holy days, sin offerings, and the priesthood. Since God singled out the tribe of **LEVI** to be priests and since this book contains those detailed instructions for the priests, it is called **LEVI**ticus.

THE 5 POETICAL BOOKS

JOB

"THE PROBLEM OF HUMAN SUFFERING"

PSALMS

"AN ANATOMY OF ALL PARTS OF THE SOUL AND A MIRROR REFLECTING EVERY POSSIBLE MOVEMENT OF MAN'S SPIRIT"

PROVERBS

"UNDERSTANDING AND PRACTICING WISDOM BASED ON GOD'S LAW"

SONG OF SOLOMON

"LOVE OF HUMAN HEARTS AND GOD'S LOVE FOR HIS PEOPLE"

ECCLESIASTES

"SOLVING THE RIDDLE OF MAN'S EXISTENCE"

In order to get a good, clear understanding of the seventeen prophetical books, it is important to know **when** and **to whom** each book is directed. If a person does not know that, it will be almost impossible to understand the message of the prophets.

There are two things that can really help you remember **when** each prophet prophesied. The first of these two is to simply know that **all seventeen of the prophets' messages *revolve rather closely around the Exile* -- they all took place either *DURING* the exile, a short time *BEFORE*, or a short time *AFTER*.** The chart on the following page shows when each prophet's message fits in relation to the Exile.

THE PROPHETS (*WHEN* THEY PROPHESIED)

MAJOR PROPHETS

ISAIAH
JEREMIAH
LAMENTATIONS
EZEKIEL
DANIEL

MINOR PROPHETS

HOSEA
JOEL
AMOS
OBADIAH
JONAH
MICAH
NAHUM
HABAKKUK
ZEPHANIAH
HAGGAI
ZECHARIAH
MALACHI

*The last three MAJOR PROPHETS' messages were **during** the Exile. The last three MINOR PROPHETS' messages were **after** the Exile. All others were **before** the Exile.*

The second thing that will help you remember **when** each one prophesied is to know that **"politically" all seventeen revolve around the *emerging and reign of three world powers.*** Those three world powers were:

1. The Assyrian Empire.
2. The Babylonian Empire.
3. The Persian Empire.

As for **who** the messages were directed to, the chart on the following page gives a good, simple way to remember that.

THE PROPHETS (*TO WHOM* THEY PROPHESIED)

The messages of ALL BUT FIVE of the prophets were to the southern kingdom of JUDAH.

You can then take the first letter of the five whose message was to someone other than Judah and *spell the word JONAH.*

PROPHET	MESSAGE DIRECTED TO:
J - Jonah	***Nineveh* -- actually to Israel's enemy, Assyria, because Nineveh was the capital of Assyria.**
O - Obadiah	***Edom* -- The nation that had refused passage to Israel while on journey from Egypt.**
N - Nahum	***Nineveh***
A - Amos	***The northern kingdom of Israel.***
H - Hosea	***The northern kingdom of Israel.***

Assignment For This Chapter

1. Give a good way to remember the basic contents of the following three books.

Genesis: ______________________________

____

Exodus: ______________________________

____

Numbers: ______________________________

____

2. Give the name of the leader whose story is found in each of the following books.

BOOK	LEADER
JOSHUA	
JUDGES	
I SAMUEL	
II SAMUEL	
I KINGS	
II KINGS	
EZRA	
NEHEMIAH	

3. Give a good way to remember the basic contents of each of the following books.

Deuteronomy: ____

____

1 Chronicles: ____

____

2 Chronicles: ____

____

Ruth: ____

____

Esther: ____

____

Leviticus: ____

____

Job: ____

____

Psalms: ____

____

Proverbs: ____

____

Ecclesiastes: ____

____

Song of Solomon: ____

____

4. Name the prophetical books whose message was given during the following periods:

BEFORE the Exile

1. ______
2. ______
3. ______
4. ______
5. ______
6. ______
7. ______
8. ______
9. ______
10. ______
11. ______

DURING the Exile

1. ______
2. ______
3. ______

AFTER the Exile

1. ______
2. ______
3. ______

5. The message of all seventeen prophetical books was given during the emerging and reign of three world powers. Those three world powers are:

   1.______________________________

   2.______________________________

   3.______________________________

6. The message of all but the following five prophets was to Judah. Fill in the blanks to show to whom the message of those five was directed.

J onah ______________________

O badiah ______________________

N ahum ______________________

A mos ______________________

H osea ______________________

Eight Quick And Easy Ways To Get A Clear-Focused Overview Of The Entire Old Testament

STEP NUMBER 6:

God's Seven Major Covenants With Man

GOD'S SEVEN MAJOR COVENANTS WITH MAN

Another excellent way to get a good, clear overall picture of the structure and framework of the Old Testament is to become familiar with the seven major covenants that God has made with man and then **remember them in sequence.**

The book of Hebrews points out that "many times and in various ways" God has spoken to mankind. Many, many times, He has **divinely intervened, revealed Himself, and EVEN made covenants with His creation.** Of those, there are **seven absolutely major covenants** that when taken as a whole give a great deal of the story of God's message to mankind. Simply by understanding the content of these seven covenants, you will have a "bird's-eye view" of the entire Bible. **AND simply by remembering them in sequence,** you will have a good chronological structure in your mind; **because these seven covenants give the "flow of history" and the "flow of the Bible."** They give chronology, structure, framework, skeleton.

These covenants also clearly distinguish the Christian religion from that of all others, because they clearly demonstrate **one of the most basic facts of Christianity . . . . .**

It is God Himself who INITIATES the contact between God and man.

In every religion, you have the story of man's search for God (by whatever name they call Him). **BUT . . . . .**

In Christianity you not only have the story of MAN'S SEARCH FOR GOD; you also have the story of GOD'S SEARCH FOR MAN.

That fact is nowhere more clearly displayed than in the covenants (agreements, contracts) that He has made with man. **In each case, it was God who sought out man with whom to make the agreement.**

The seven major covenants that God has made with man are:

1. **The Edenic Covenant**
2. **The Adamic Covenant**
3. **The Noahic Covenant**
4. **The Abrahamic Covenant**
5. **The Mosaic Covenant**
6. **The Davidic Covenant**
7. **The New Covenant**

Let's briefly examine each of them. Be sure that you know the general content of each covenant, and then after you have a clear understanding of each one, simply memorize the sequence of these seven covenants; and once again you will have a way to in total darkness go through the entire Old Testament in skeleton form.

The Edenic Covenant

It all began, obviously, when God placed Adam and Eve in the Garden of Eden. Made in the image of God, they became responsible to subdue the earth, to have dominion over all living things, and replenish the earth with generations like themselves.

If they had kept their part of the Edenic Covenant they would have lived and not died. However, they failed in their part of the covenant. Because of their disobedience sin entered, bringing with it man's fall and death, which afterwards would touch all of mankind.

The Adamic Covenant

After Adam sinned, God did not abandon His plan for mankind. Instead, He made a second covenant with **Adam.** This second covenant is known as **The Adamic Covenant, and it sets forth the conditions that now exist in the life of *Fallen Mankind.*** These conditions include: (1) motherhood linked with pain and sorrow; (2) the earth cursed to bring forth thorns and thistles; (3) burdensome labor required; and (4) physical death touching all of mankind. However, along with the curses placed upon the earth and upon man, God gave the first promise of a Redeemer (Genesis 3:15).

The Noahic Covenant

The entrance of sin wrought havoc upon man. In the generations following the Fall of Man, one individual after another succumbed to Satan. One of the few bright spots during this period was Enoch who faithfully "walked with God" (Genesis 5:24). Most all others walked in wickedness.

Because of the terrible wickedness of this multiplying race, God determined to destroy man from the face of the Earth. "But **Noah** found grace in the eyes of the Lord" (Genesis 6:8); and God made a covenant with him through which sinful man would, indeed, be destroyed and then the earth be replenished through Noah and his family. This is **The Noahic Covenant.**

The Abrahamic Covenant

The next major covenant that God made was **THE ABRAHAMIC COVENANT** found in Genesis 12:1-3. Here, God singles out one man -- **ABRAHAM** -- and promises to do two things. He promises in verse two to "make . . . a great nation" of Abraham, and in verse three He promises to bless all families of the earth through Abraham's "seed."

These three verses covering the Abrahamic Covenant **are the very pivot point** of the Old Testament, and **an understanding of this covenant is absolutely essential if a person is going to have a good understanding of the Bible.** If a person fails to see how these three verses fit into God's Plan for the Ages, it will be impossible to thoroughly understand the Old Testament -- or the New -- **because these three verses contain, in capsule form, the whole of God's purpose and plan.**

From Genesis 12:3 onward, **the entire balance of the Old Testament is the story of this "nation" that God promised to make of Abraham, and the New Testament is the story of "all families of the earth" being blessed through Abraham's "seed."**

The Mosaic Covenant

The nation that God promised to make of Abraham began to develop; and when the "nation" had grown to a "population" of seventy, Jacob's family moved into Egypt because of the famine and because one of his sons -- Joseph -- had become ruler there.

During the 430 years they were in Egypt, **the family multiplied rapidly and did, in fact, become a mighty *nation.*** Their growth within the borders of Egypt frightened the Egyptians, and they responded with cruel oppression and bondage.

The Israelites cried to God for deliverance, and He raised up **MOSES** to lead them from the Bondage of Egypt back home to the Promised Land.

While on that journey, at Mt. Sinai, God made a covenant with the people through Moses. It is known as **THE MOSAIC COVENANT.**

The Davidic Covenant

After Joshua's death and the 400 year period of the Judges, God established **His kingdom covenant with DAVID.** This is known as **the Davidic Covenant.** In this covenant, God promised David that his seed would continually be "king." The ultimate fulfillment of that promise, of course, was Jesus -- The King of kings -- who came through the seed and lineage of David.

The New Covenant

God proved faithful through each of these covenants and kept the promise of the "seed" alive. Then when Christ was born, all of these previous covenants converged and merged in **the New Covenant.** This covenant is embodied in the life and teachings of Jesus, and a study of the New Testament will unfold the content of it.

Assignment For This Chapter

1. Name the seven major covenants.
2. Give a brief description of the seven major covenants.

Edenic: ______________________________

____

____

Adamic: ______________________________

____

____

Noahic: ______________________________

____

____

Abrahamic: ______________________________

____

____

Mosaic: ______________________________

____

____

Davidic: ______________________________

____

____

The New Covenant: ______________________________

____

____

3. Read the first six major covenants directly from scripture. (See page 138.)

Eight Quick And Easy Ways To Get A Clear-Focused Overview Of The Entire Old Testament

STEP NUMBER 7:

THE FIVE MAJOR TIME PERIODS

THE FIVE MAJOR TIME PERIODS

In this chapter, the Old Testament has been divided into five major time periods; and I strongly suggest that you look at each of these five **as a unit within itself. For the time being, you are not looking at the entire Old Testament -- just that one particular time period.** Be sure that you know what was going on during that one unit--who the key people were, the major events, and the general flow of what God was doing during that period of time. After you have a good, clear mental picture of what was going on, you can move on to the next time period, and to the next until you can see all five of them clearly in your mind. You will then have the entire Old Testament **in five neat packages that will be very easy to learn and very easy to remember. The five time periods referred to in this chapter are:**

1. BEFORE ISRAEL BECAME A NATION.
(This covers the entire period of time from creation through the flood, the call of Abraham, the beginning

growth of Abraham's family until the "nation" had reached the "population" of 70 and Joseph had been sold into Egypt).

2. **ISRAEL IN EGYPT.**

   (The next 430 years. During this period the "nation" grew from only 70 to more than two million).

3. **ISRAEL IN THE WILDERNESS.**

   (The next 40 years -- from the miraculous crossing of the Red Sea, through the 40 years of wilderness wanderings, until the miraculous crossing of the Jordan River).

4. **BACK IN THE PROMISED LAND.**

   (Approximately 1,000 years. This period includes the conquest and dividing of Canaan, the remainder of Joshua's lifetime, the 400 year period of the Judges, the time of the United Kingdom and the Divided Kingdom until Israel was scattered by the Assyrians and Judah was carried captive to Babylon by Nebuchadnezzar).

5. **THE EXILE AND BEYOND.**

   (The 70 years of Exile, the return to Jerusalem, and Jewish history afterwards).

In order to be sure that you have all five of the time periods clearly in your mind **in five neat packages,** spend some time reviewing the charts on the following pages.

TIME PERIOD NUMBER ONE:

BEFORE ISRAEL BECAME A NATION

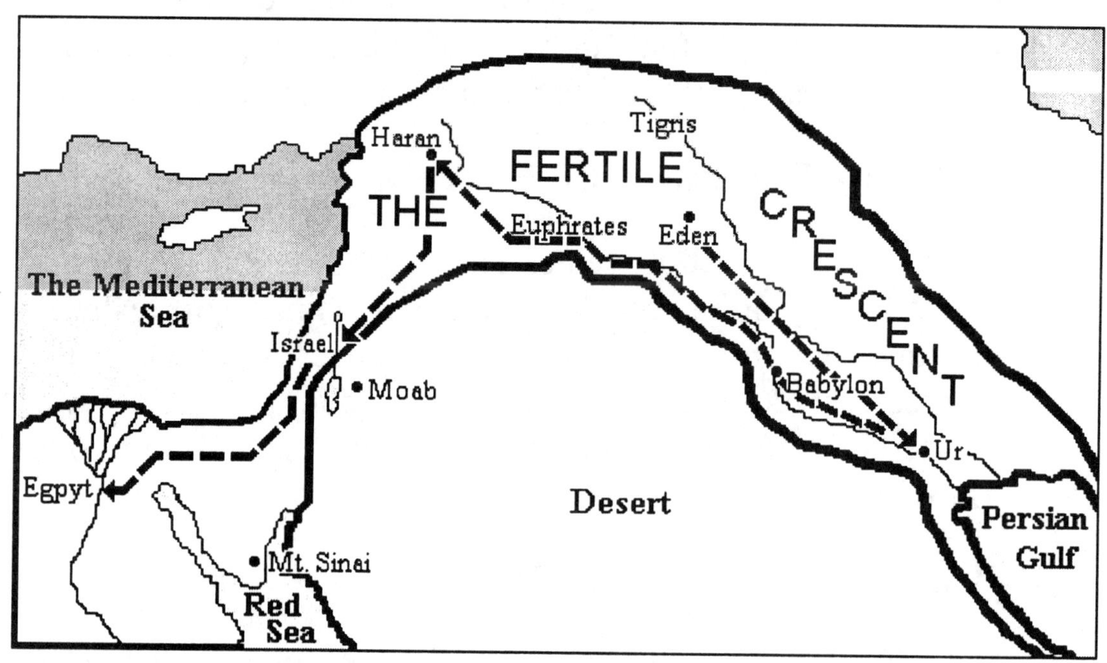

(FROM CREATION TO JOSEPH'S DEATH IN EGYPT)

BEFORE ISRAEL BECAME A NATION

KEY PEOPLE:

1. Adam
2. Noah
3. Abraham
4. Isaac
5. Jacob
6. Joseph

BOOK WHERE STORY IS FOUND:

1. Genesis

MAJOR MOVES:

1. Eden to Ur
2. Ur to Haran
3. Haran to Israel
4. Israel to Egypt

MAJOR COVENANTS:

1. The Edenic Covenant
2. The Adamic Covenant
3. The Noahic Covenant
4. The Abrahamic Covenant

TIME PERIOD NUMBER TWO:

ISRAEL IN EGYPT

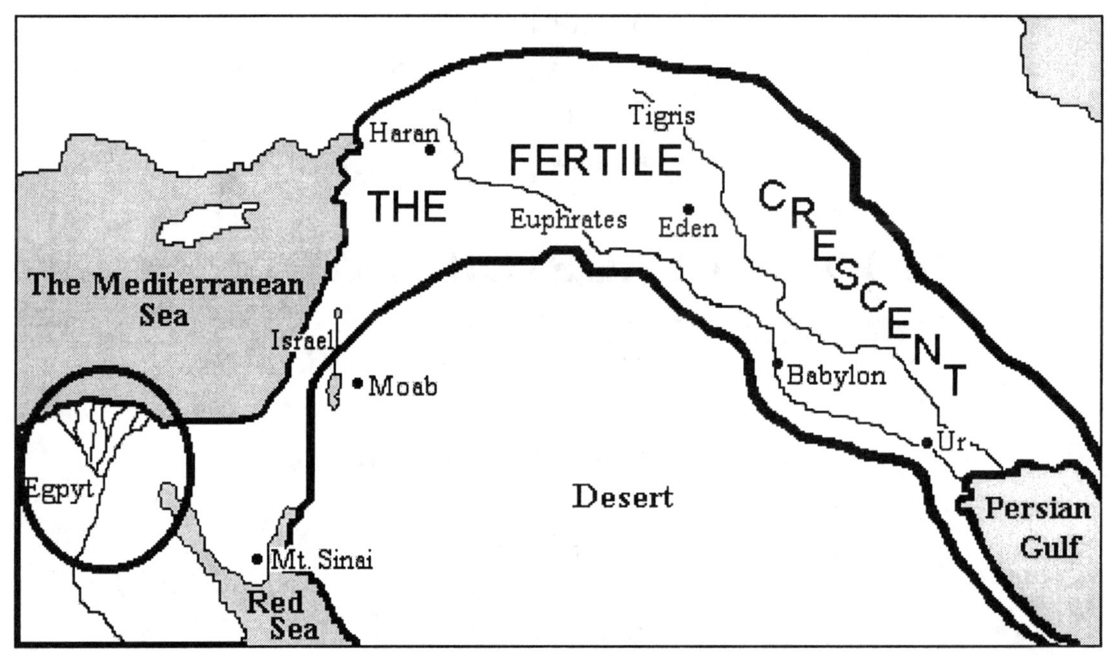

(THE NEXT 430 YEARS)

ISRAEL IN EGYPT

KEY PEOPLE:

1. Moses
2. Pharaoh

BOOK WHERE STORY IS FOUND:

1. Exodus

MAJOR MOVE:

1. Egypt back to Canaan
   (The move was begun
   during this period)

ISRAEL'S LEADER:

1. Moses

TIME PERIOD NUMBER THREE:

ISRAEL IN THE WILDERNESS

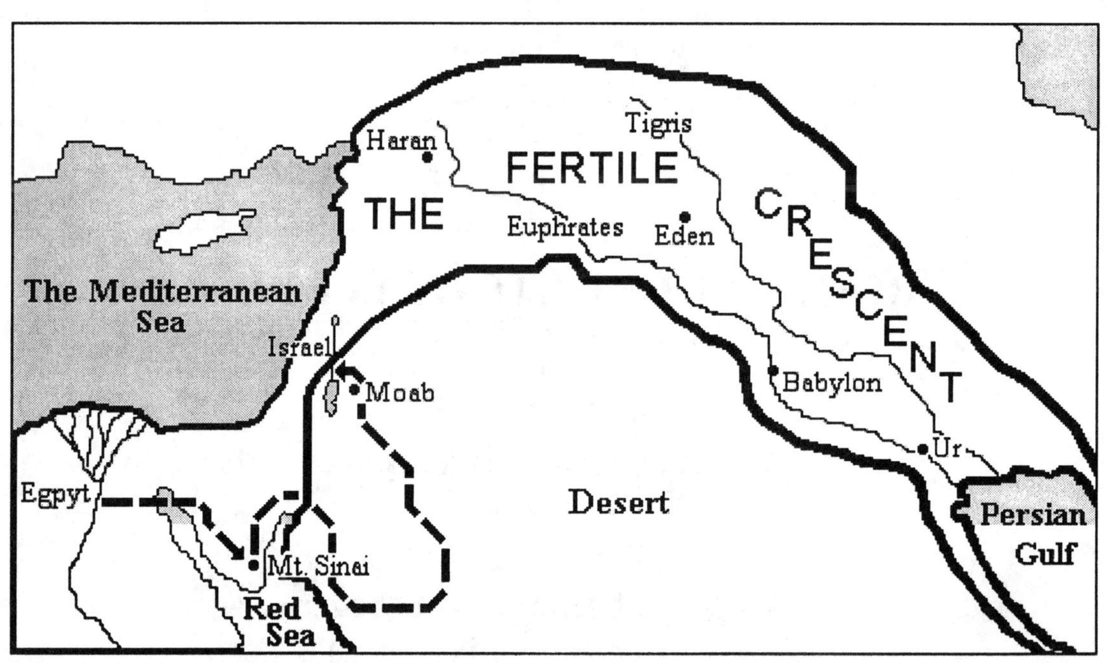

(THE NEXT 40 YEARS)

ISRAEL IN THE WILDERNESS

KEY PEOPLE:

1. Moses

BOOKS WHERE STORY IS FOUND:

1. Exodus (last part)
2. Numbers

MAJOR MOVE:

1. Egypt Back to Canaan
   (the move was in progress
   the entire 40 years)

ISRAEL'S LEADER:

1. Moses

MAJOR COVENANT:

1. The Mosaic Covenant

TIME PERIOD NUMBER FOUR:

BACK IN THE PROMISED LAND

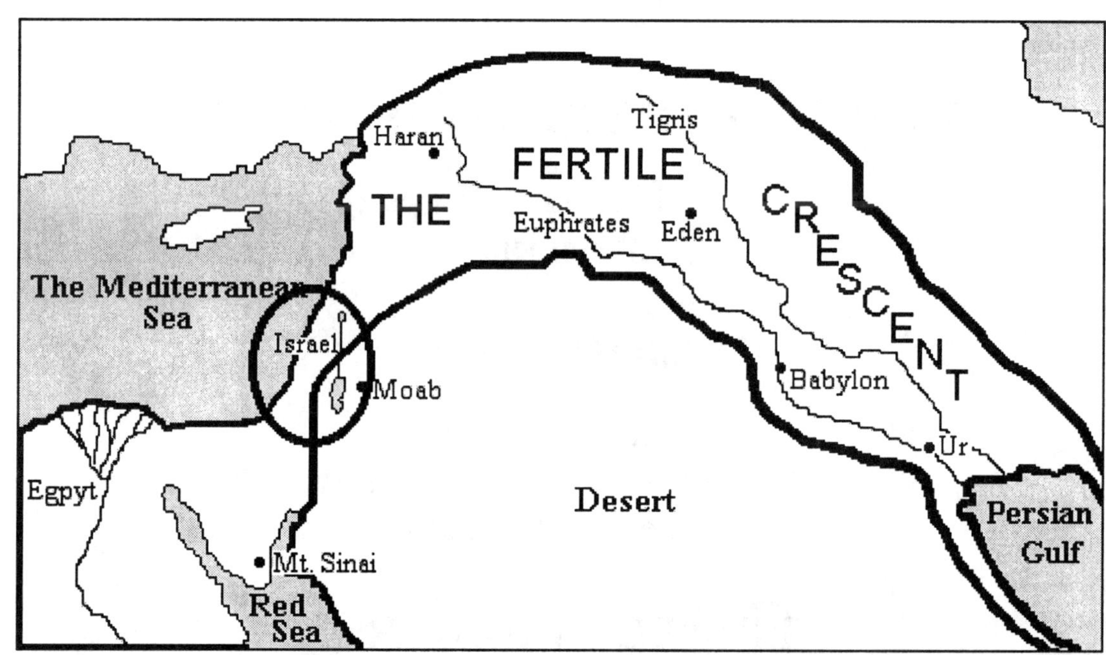

(APPROXIMATELY THE NEXT 1,000 YEARS)

BACK IN THE PROMISED LAND

KEY PEOPLE:

1. Joshua
2. The Twelve Judges
3. Samuel
4. Saul
5. David
6. Solomon
7. The 39 Kings of the Divided Kingdom
8. The Prophets

BOOKS WHERE STORY IS FOUND:

1. Joshua
2. Judges
3. I & II Samuel
4. I & II Kings

ISRAEL'S LEADERS:

1. Joshua
2. The Twelve Judges
3. Samuel
4. Saul
5. David
6. Solomon
7. The 39 Kings of the Divided Kingdom

MAJOR COVENANT:

1. The Davidic Covenant

TIME PERIOD NUMBER FIVE:

THE EXILE AND BEYOND

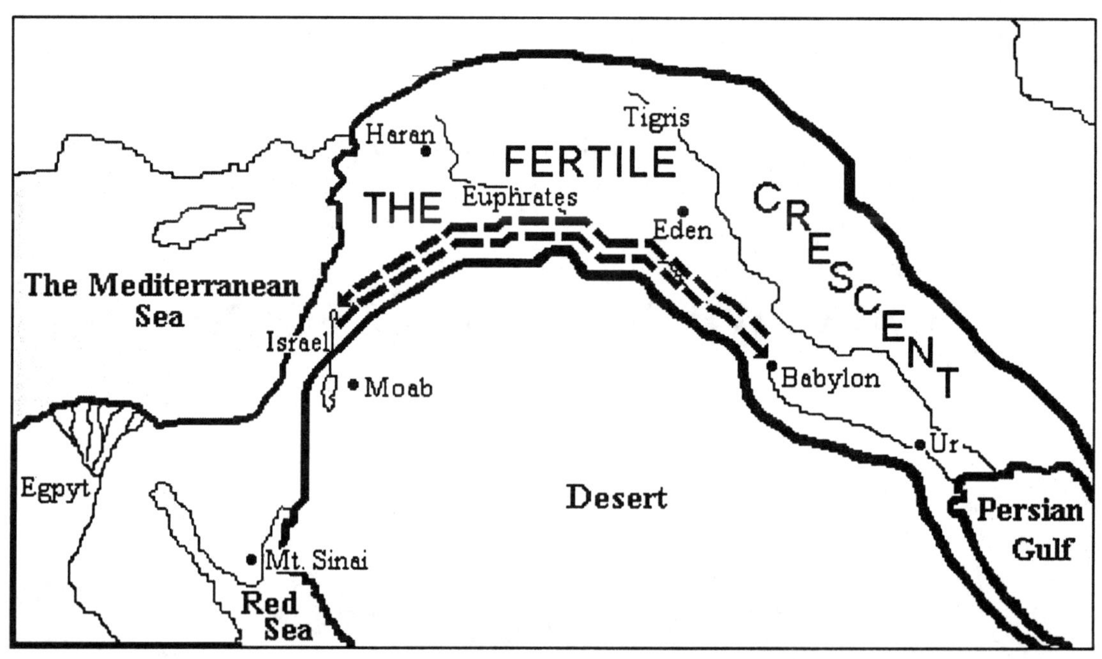

(THE 70 YEARS OF EXILE, THE RETURN TO JERUSALEM, AND JEWISH HISTORY AFTER THE EXILE)

THE EXILE AND BEYOND

KEY PEOPLE:

1. Nebuchadnezzar
2. The Prophets
3. Zerubbabel
4. Ezra
5. Nehemiah

BOOKS WHERE STORY IS FOUND:

1. II Kings (last part)
2. Ezra
3. Nehemiah
4. (also Daniel & Ezekiel)

MAJOR MOVES:

1. Jerusalem to Babylon
2. Babylon Back to Jerusalem

ISRAEL'S LEADERS:

1. Zerubbabel
2. Ezra
3. Nehemiah

THE FIVE MAJOR TIME PERIODS

1. **BEFORE ISRAEL BECAME A NATION**
   (From creation to Joseph's death in Egypt)

2. **ISRAEL IN EGYPT**
   (The next 430 years)

3. **ISRAEL IN THE WILDERNESS**
   (The next 40 years)

4. **BACK IN THE PROMISED LAND**
   (The next approximately 1,000 years from the crossing of the Jordan until the Exile)

5. **THE EXILE AND BEYOND**
   (The 70 years of Exile, the return to Jerusalem, and Jewish history afterward)

Assignment For This Chapter

1. Name the five major time periods of the Old Testament. (Use separate sheet.)

2. Give a brief description of each time period.

   1. Before Israel Became a Nation: ____________________
   ____
   ____
   ____

   2. Israel in Egypt: ____________________
   ____
   ____
   ____

   3. Israel in the Wilderness: ____________________
   ____
   ____
   ____

   4. Back in the Promised Land: ____________________
   ____
   ____
   ____

   5. The Exile and Beyond: ____________________
   ____
   ____
   ____

3. Identify the book or books where the story of each of the time periods is found. (Use separate sheet.)

Eight Quick And Easy Ways To Get A Clear-Focused Overview Of The Entire Old Testament

STEP NUMBER 8:

The Fifty Major Events Of The Old Testament

THE FIFTY MAJOR EVENTS OF THE OLD TESTAMENT

Finally, we will look at the fifty major events of the Old Testament. If you were to meet someone today that you had never seen before and they told you the fifty major events of their life, you would probably know more about that person than you do about most of the people you have known for years.

In like manner, you will be able to learn much about the Old Testament simply by becoming familiar with the major events recorded in it. So, I have chosen what I consider to be the fifty major events of the Old Testament; and you will find them listed on the following pages.

Knowing these fifty events will give you a clear, distinct TRAIL through the entire Old Testament. If there are any of the events that you are not completely familiar with, spend whatever time it takes to become familiar with each of these fifty. After doing that, review these pages often enough for you to get the "flow" of these events and to be able to remember them in sequence.

In order to make it much easier for you to do that, **the events have been divided into the five major time periods** discussed in the previous chapter. That way, you do not have fifty things to remember in one group. The maximum number in any group is fourteen.

Over the next few weeks take the "groupings" that are found in this chapter and throughout the book and **focus on them one "grouping" at a time until each is firmly in your mind and until you can "travel" through every one of them without a single "bump."**

By taking them one "grouping" at a time, it will be **far easier than you may have thought.** You will find that by following this procedure, **it truly makes the Old Testament Simple.**

BEFORE ISRAEL BECAME A NATION

1. **The Creation**
2. **The Fall of Man**
3. **The Flood**
4. **The Beginning of Nations and Languages**
5. **The Call of Abraham**
6. **The Birth of Isaac**
7. **The Birth of Jacob**
8. **Jacob's Name Changed to Israel**
9. **Twelve Sons Born to Jacob**
10. **Joseph Sold into Egypt**
11. **Jacob's Family Moves to Egypt**

ISRAEL IN EGYPT

1. **Jacob's Family Becomes a Nation**
2. **"There Arises a Pharoah Who Knew Not Joseph"**
3. **Moses is Born**
4. **The Burning Bush**
5. **Moses Sent to Pharaoh**
6. **The Ten Plagues**
7. **The Passover**
8. **The Exodus**

ISRAEL IN THE WILDERNESS

1. **The Law at Mt. Sinai**
2. **The Tabernacle**
3. **The Twelve Spies Sent into Canaan**
4. **Wilderness Wanderings**
5. **The New Generation taught at Moab**
6. **Joshua Succeeds Moses**

BACK IN THE PROMISED LAND

1. The Crossing of Jordan
2. The Land Divided Among the Twelve Tribes
3. The Time of the Judges
4. Ruth Follows Naomi into Canaan
5. The Ministry of Samuel
6. Israel Demands a King
7. Saul Anointed King
8. David Becomes King
9. Solomon Becomes King
10. The Temple Built
11. The Kingdom Divided
12. The Ministry of Elijah
13. The Ministry of Elisha
14. The Prophets Warn Israel and Judah

THE EXILE AND BEYOND

1. **Assyria Scatters Israel**
2. **Babylon Carries Judah Captive**
3. **Ezekiel's Vision**
4. **Shadrach, Meshach, & Abednego Thrown into the Fiery Furnace**
5. **Daniel Thrown into the Lion's Den**
6. **Persia Overthrows the Babylonian Kingdom**
7. **Judah Returns to Jerusalem**
8. **Esther Becomes Queen**
9. **The Prophecies of Haggai, Zechariah, & Malachi**
10. **The Silent Years**
11. **The Birth of Christ**

Assignment For This Chapter

1. Name the fifty major events of the Old Testament by filling in the blanks below.

Before Israel Became a Nation

1. ______________________________
2. ______________________________
3. ______________________________
4. ______________________________
5. ______________________________
6. ______________________________
7. ______________________________
8. ______________________________
9. ______________________________
10. ______________________________
11. ______________________________

Israel in Egypt

1. ______________________________
2. ______________________________
3. ______________________________
4. ______________________________
5. ______________________________
6. ______________________________
7. ______________________________
8. ______________________________

Israel in the Wilderness

1. ______________________________
2. ______________________________
3. ______________________________

4. ____________________
5. ____________________
6. ____________________

Back in the Promised Land

1. ____________________
2. ____________________
3. ____________________
4. ____________________
5. ____________________
6. ____________________
7. ____________________
8. ____________________
9. ____________________
10. ____________________
11. ____________________
12. ____________________
13. ____________________
14. ____________________

The Exile and Beyond

1. ____________________
2. ____________________
3. ____________________
4. ____________________
5. ____________________
6. ____________________
7. ____________________
8. ____________________
9. ____________________
10. ____________________
11. ____________________

2. Read the story of the fifty major events **directly from scripture.** (See page 138-139.)

TYING IT ALL TOGETHER (PROMPTER SHEETS)

The following five pages are prompter sheets which you can use to be sure that you remember the key people, the major events, the major moves, Israel's leader/leaders, the major covenants, and the book/books where the story for each of the five time periods is found. I suggest that you not actually fill in the pages but that you leave them blank so that you can continue reviewing them from time to time until they are firmly in your mind. By doing that, the framework and skeleton will be yours to keep forever.

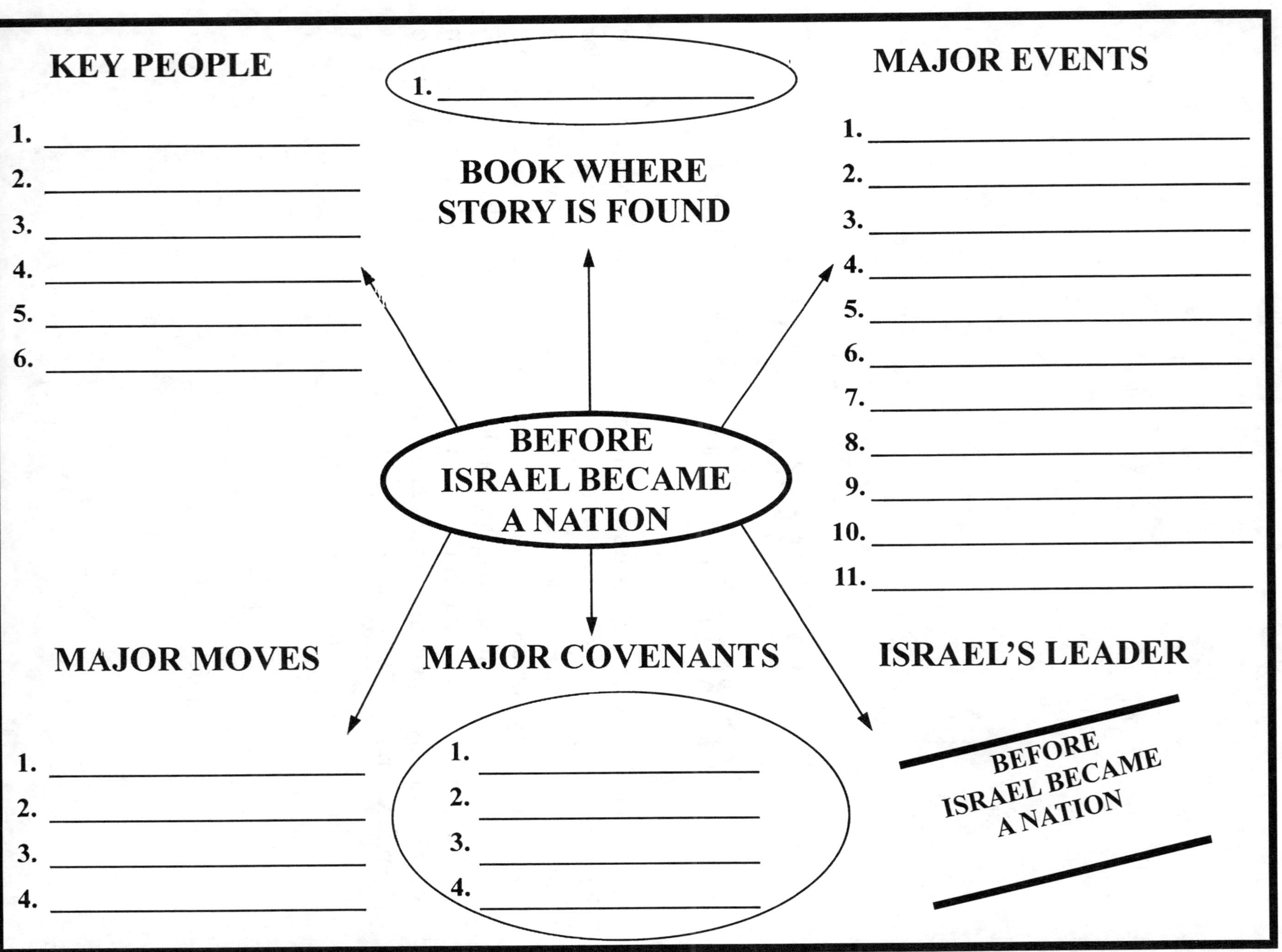
KEY PEOPLE
1.
2.
3.
4.
5.
6.
1.
BOOK WHERE STORY IS FOUND
MAJOR EVENTS
1.
2.
3.
4.
5.
6.
7.
8.
9.
10.
11.
BEFORE ISRAEL BECAME A NATION
MAJOR MOVES
1.
2.
3.
4.
MAJOR COVENANTS
1.
2.
3.
4.
ISRAEL'S LEADER
BEFORE ISRAEL BECAME A NATION

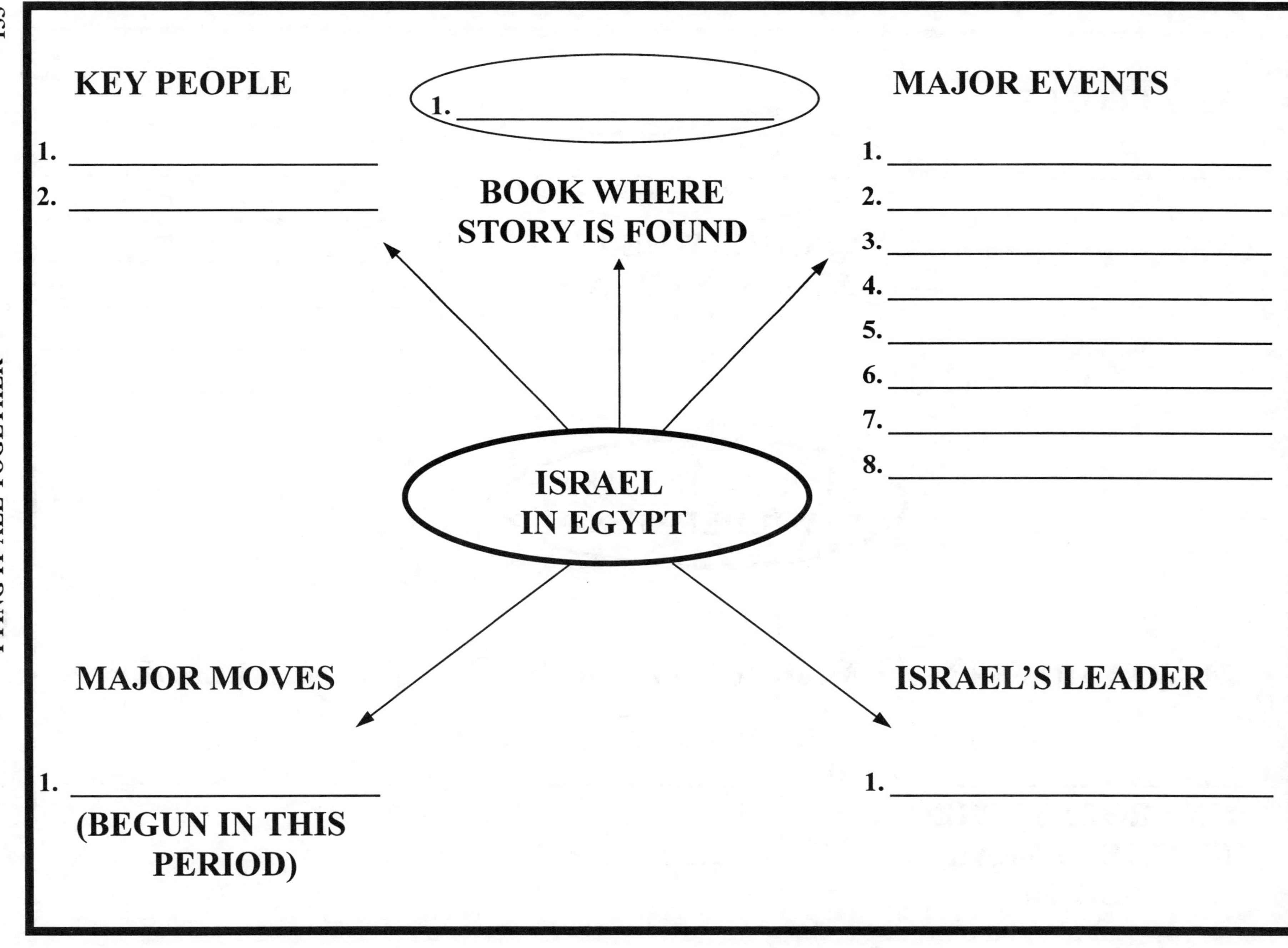
KEY PEOPLE
1. ____
2. ____
1. ____
BOOK WHERE STORY IS FOUND
MAJOR EVENTS
1. ____
2. ____
3. ____
4. ____
5. ____
6. ____
7. ____
8. ____
ISRAEL IN EGYPT
MAJOR MOVES
1. ____
(BEGUN IN THIS PERIOD)
ISRAEL'S LEADER
1. ____

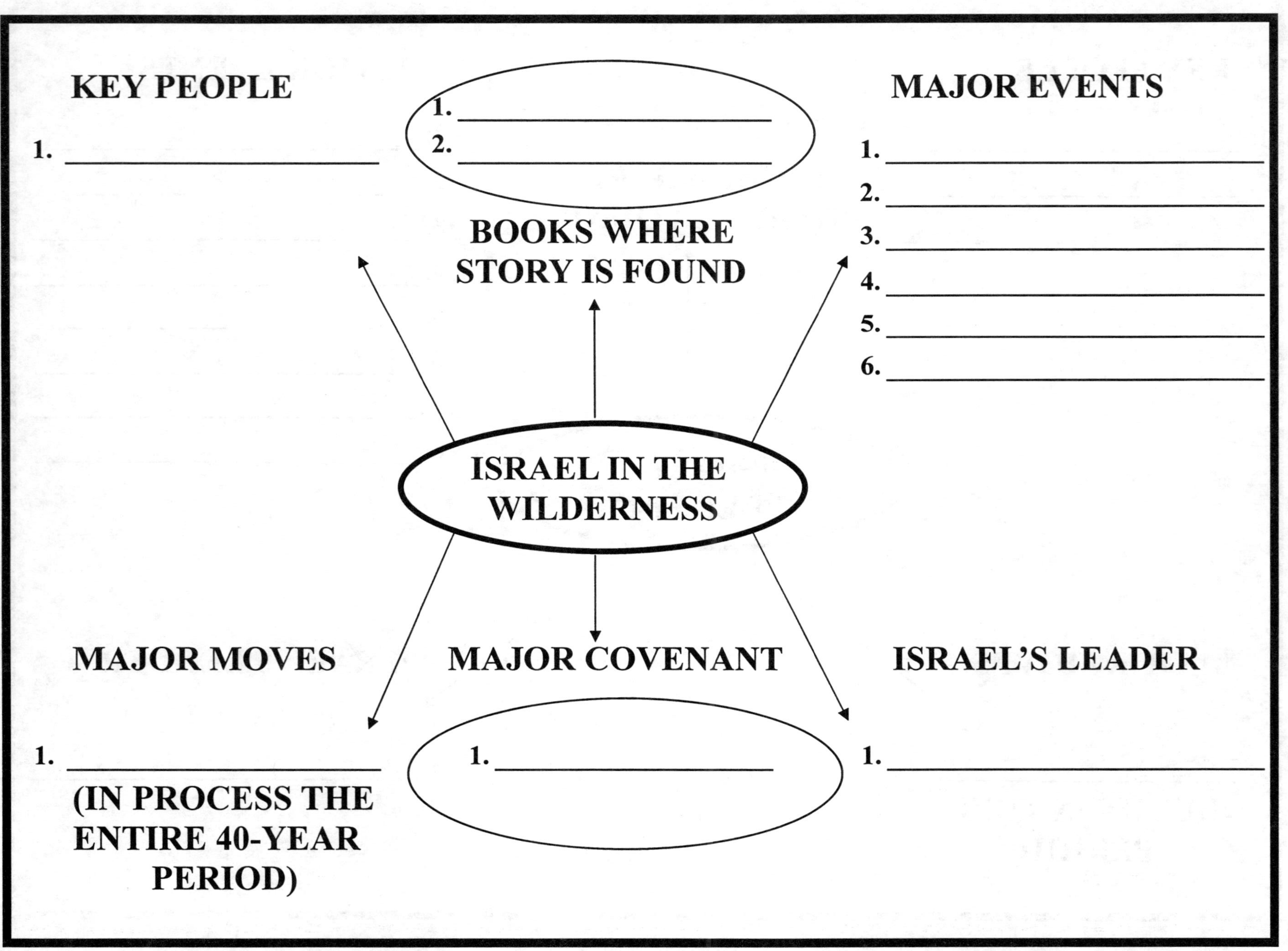
KEY PEOPLE
1.
BOOKS WHERE STORY IS FOUND
1.
2.
MAJOR EVENTS
1.
2.
3.
4.
5.
6.
ISRAEL IN THE WILDERNESS
MAJOR MOVES
1.
(IN PROCESS THE ENTIRE 40-YEAR PERIOD)
MAJOR COVENANT
1.
ISRAEL'S LEADER
1.

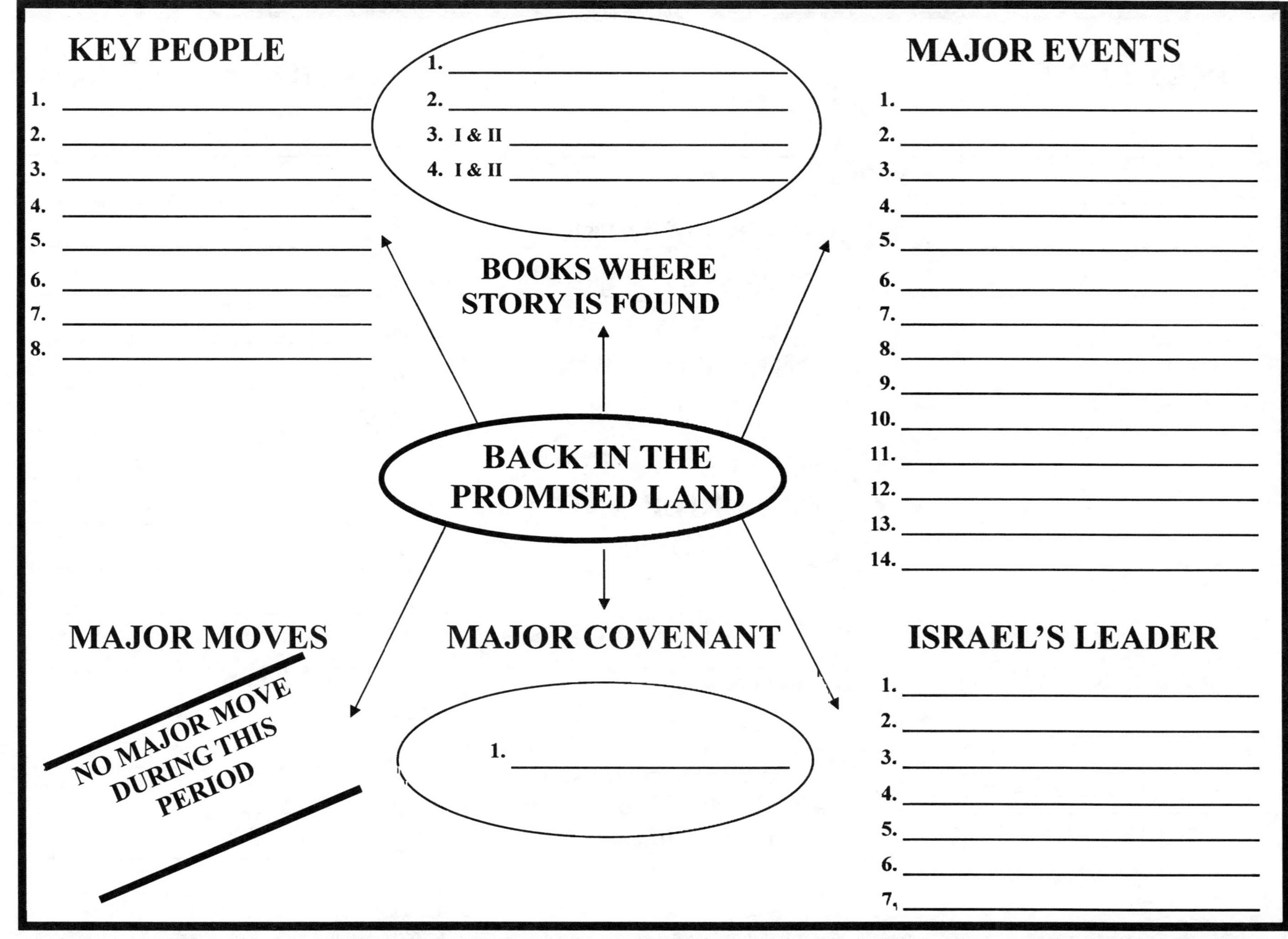
KEY PEOPLE
1.
2.
3.
4.
5.
6.
7.
8.
1.
2.
3. I & II
4. I & II
BOOKS WHERE STORY IS FOUND
MAJOR EVENTS
1.
2.
3.
4.
5.
6.
7.
8.
9.
10.
11.
12.
13.
14.
BACK IN THE PROMISED LAND
MAJOR MOVES
NO MAJOR MOVE DURING THIS PERIOD
MAJOR COVENANT
1.
ISRAEL'S LEADER
1.
2.
3.
4.
5.
6.
7.

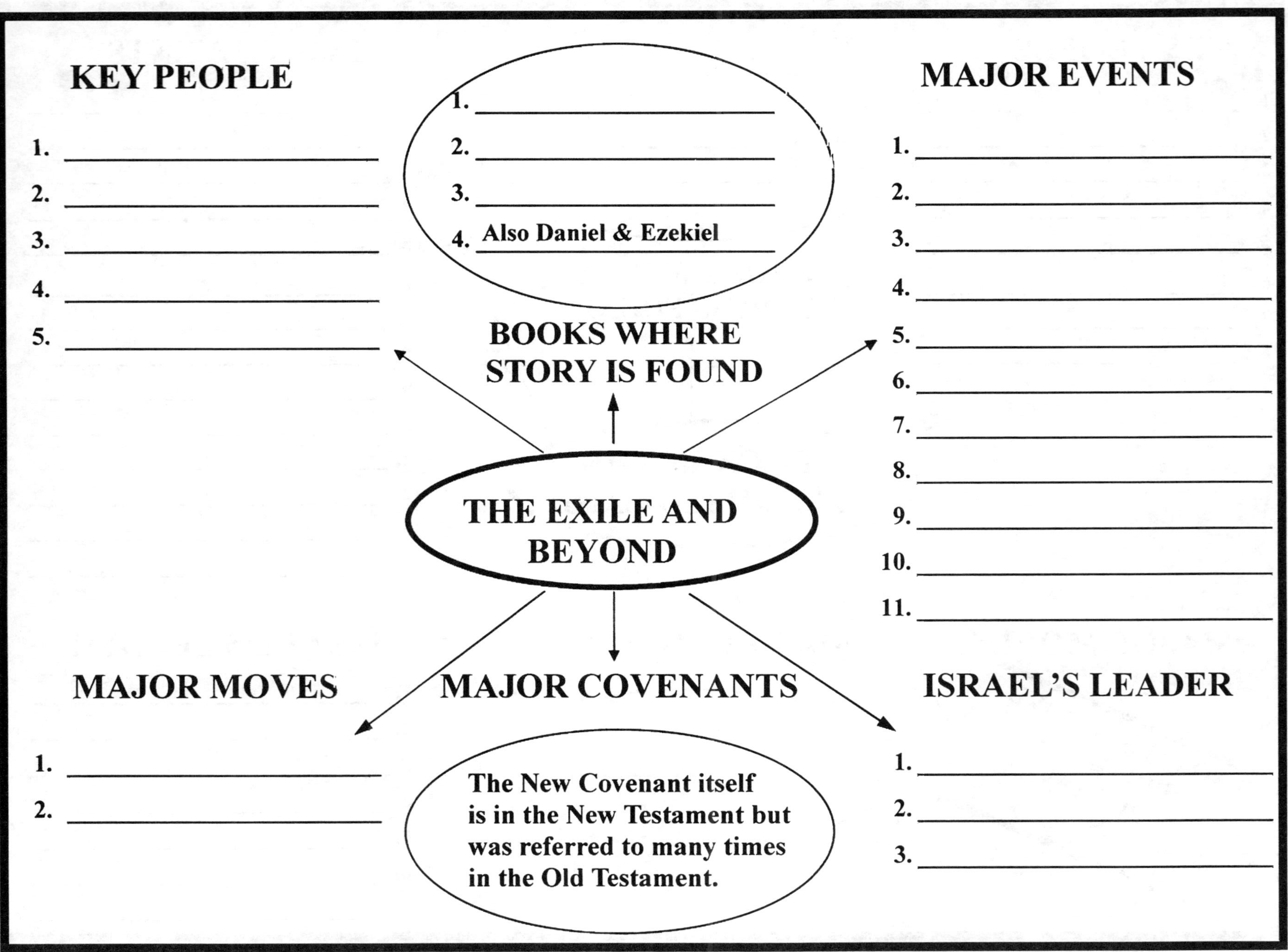
KEY PEOPLE
1.
2.
3.
4.
5.
1.
2.
3.
4. Also Daniel & Ezekiel
BOOKS WHERE STORY IS FOUND
MAJOR EVENTS
1.
2.
3.
4.
5.
6.
7.
8.
9.
10.
11.
THE EXILE AND BEYOND
MAJOR MOVES
1.
2.
MAJOR COVENANTS
The New Covenant itself is in the New Testament but was referred to many times in the Old Testament.
ISRAEL'S LEADER
1.
2.
3.

SCRIPTURAL REFERENCES

SCRIPTURAL REFERENCES

By now, you probably have noticed that there are almost no scriptural references made in the previous chapters. **This was intentional**. They were left out because the concept **"calls"** for them to **temporarily** be left out.

The very first principle of the concept is to take each of the eight categories -- one at a time -- and strip away every single detail that can possibly be stripped away, leaving only the bare minimum facts that must be left for the reader to get a good, clear, overall picture of that particular approach.

By having only 5, 7, 11, or some other small number of things, it will be very easy to get a good, thorough knowledge of that entire category. Once all eight **"blocks"** have been covered, **they can then be merged back into** the total picture.

Once you have done that, I strongly suggest that you review them again -- this time also covering the scriptural reference for each particular item.

To help you do that, you will find a listing below of some of the primary scriptural references covering items listed in the previous chapters of this book.

THE SEVEN MAJOR MOVES

MOVE NUMBER 1: Gen. 3:23-24; 10:8-12, 19, 30; 11:2-9, 26-28

MOVE NUMBER 2: Gen 11:31-32.

MOVE NUMBER 3: Gen 12:1-9.

MOVE NUMBER 4: Gen 37:1-36; 41:14 - 47:12.

MOVE NUMBER 5: Ex. 1:1 - 14:31. The remaining travels during the next 40 years are detailed in the remainder of Exodus and the book of Numbers. They are also summarized in the book of Deuteronomy. Joshua 1:1 through 4:24 then covers the actual entry into the Promised Land.

MOVE NUMBER 6: 2 Kings 24:1 - 25:21; 2 Chron. 36:5-21.

MOVE NUMBER 7: 2 Chron. 36:22-23; Ezra 1:1 - 2:70.

THE TWENTY KEY PEOPLE (OR GROUPS OF PEOPLE)

1. ADAM: Gen. 1:26-31; 2:7 - 5:5.

2. NOAH: Gen 5:28 - 9:29

3. ABRAHAM: Gen 11:26 - 25:10.

4. ISAAC: Gen. 21:1 - 28:9

5. JACOB: Gen. 25:19 - 35:29; 37:1-36; 42:1 - 50:13.

6. JOSEPH: Gen. 30:22-25; 37:1-36; 39:1 - 50:26

7. MOSES: Ex. 1:6 - Deut. 34:12.

8. JOSHUA: God's grooming of Joshua is found throughout the books covering the story of Moses (listed above) and then the story of his own leadership is found throughout the book of Joshua.

9. THE TWELVE JUDGES: The book of Judges.

10. SAMUEL: 1 Sam. 1:1 - 25:1

11. SAUL: 1 Sam. 9:1 - 31:13

12. DAVID: God's choice and grooming of David is found from 1 Samuel 16:1 throughout the remainder of 1 Samuel; his reign as king is found in the book of 2 Samuel; and his old age and death is found in 1 Kings 1:1 - 2:12.

13. SOLOMON: 2 Sam. 12:24; 1 Kings 1:1 - 11:43.

14. THE 39 KINGS OF THE DIVIDED KINGDOM: 1 Kings 12:1 - 2 Kings 25:30.

15. ZERUBBABEL: Ezra 1:1 - 6:22.

16. EZRA: Ezra 7:1 - 10:44

17. NEHEMIAH: The book of Nehemiah.

18. PHARAOH: Gen. 40:1 - Ex. 14:31

19. NEBUCHADNEZZAR: 2 Kings 24:1 - 25:30; Jer. 27:6 - 29:14; Dan. 1:1 - 5:31

20. THE PROPHETS: All of the prophets fit into the time period of 1 & 2 Kings, Ezra, and Nehemiah. Each of their messages is found in the books from Isaiah through Malachi.

GOD'S SEVEN MAJOR COVENANTS

1. THE EDENIC COVENANT: Gen. 2:15-25.

2. THE ADAMIC COVENANT: Gen 3:9-19.

3. THE NOAHIC COVENANT: Gen. 6:6-22.

4. THE ABRAHAMIC COVENANT: Gen. 12:1-3.

5. THE MOSAIC COVENANT: Ex. 19:1 - 31:18.

6. THE DAVIDIC COVENANT: 1 Sam. 16:1-13, 2 Sam. 7:8-16.

7. THE NEW COVENANT: The new covenant is embodied in the life and teachings of Jesus and is found in the first four books of the New Testament.

THE FIVE MAJOR TIME PERIODS

1. BEFORE ISRAEL BECAME A NATION: The entire book of Genesis and the first six verses of Exodus. There were several stages of Israel's developing into the nation God promised to make of Abraham, but in this book I refer to them having "become a nation" at the point the ***family*** had become a very large multitude as referred to in Ex. 1:7.

2. ISRAEL IN EGYPT: Gen. 45:17 - Ex.14:31.

3. ISRAEL IN THE WILDERNESS: Ex. 16:1 - Joshua 4:19.

4. BACK IN THE PROMISED LAND: Joshua 4:19 - 2 Kings 24:10.

5. THE EXILE AND BEYOND: 2 Kings 24:11 - 25:30; Ezra - Esther; Lamentations; Ezekiel; Daniel; Haggai; Zechariah; & Malachi.

THE FIFTY MAJOR EVENTS

Before Israel Became a Nation

1. THE CREATION: Gen. 1:1 - 2:2.

2. THE FALL OF MAN: Gen. 3:1-24.

3. THE FLOOD: Gen. 6:5 - 8:22.

4. THE BEGINNING OF NATIONS AND LANGUAGES: Gen. 10:32 - 11:9.

5. THE CALL OF ABRAHAM: Gen. 12:1-3.

6. THE BIRTH OF ISAAC: Gen. 21:1-7

7. THE BIRTH OF JACOB: Gen. 25:20-26.

8. JACOB'S NAME CHANGED TO ISRAEL: Gen. 32:24-28.

9. TWELVE SONS BORN TO JACOB: Gen. 29:32 - 30:25; 35:16-19.

10. JOSEPH SOLD INTO EGYPT: Gen. 37:1-28.

11. JACOB'S FAMILY MOVES TO EGYPT: Gen. 46:1 - 47:12.

Israel in Egypt

1. JACOB'S FAMILY BECOMES A NATION: Ex. 1:7.

2. "THERE ARISES A PHARAOH WHO KNEW NOT JOSEPH.": Ex. 1:8-22.

3. MOSES IS BORN: Ex. 2:1-10

4. **THE BURNING BUSH:** Ex. 3:1 - 4:17.

5. **MOSES SENT TO PHARAOH:** Ex. 3:7-22.

6. **THE TEN PLAGUES:** Ex. 7:14 - 12:33.

7. **THE PASSOVER:** Ex. 11:1 - 12:30.

8. **THE EXODUS:** Ex. 12:30 - 14:31.

Israel in the Wilderness

1. **THE LAW AT MT. SINAI:** Ex. 19:1 - 31:18.

2. **THE TABERNACLE:** Ex. 35:4 - 40:27.

3. **THE TWELVE SPIES SENT INTO CANAAN:** Num. 13:1 - 14:45.

4. **WILDERNESS WANDERINGS:** Num. 14:11 - Deut. 34:12.

5. **THE NEW GENERATION TAUGHT AT MOAB:** Deut. 1:1 - 34:12.

6. **JOSHUA SUCCEEDS MOSES:** Deut. 34:5-12; Josh. 1:1-18.

Back in the Promised Land

1. **THE CROSSING OF JORDAN:** Josh. 3:1 - 4:24.

2. **THE LAND DIVIDED AMONG THE TWELVE TRIBES:** Josh. 13:1 - 22:9.

3. **THE TIME OF THE JUDGES:** The book of Judges.

4. **RUTH FOLLOWS NAOMI INTO CANAAN:** The book of Ruth.

5. **THE MINISTRY OF SAMUEL**: 1 Sam. 1:1 - 25:1.

6. **ISRAEL DEMANDS A KING:** 1 Sam. 8:1-21

7. **SAUL ANNOINTED KING** 1 Sam. 9:1-10:26.

8. **DAVID BECOMES KING:** 1 Sam. 16:1-13.

9. **SOLOMON BECOMES KING:** 1 Kings 1:1 - 2:12.

10. **THE TEMPLE BUILT:** 1 Kings 6:1 - 9:23.

11. **THE KINGDOM DIVIDED:** 1 Kings 12:1-19.

12. **THE MINISTRY OF ELIJAH:** 1 Kings 17:1 through the remainder of 1 Kings. His ascension is then covered in the first two chapters of 2 Kings.

13. **THE MINISTRY OF ELISHA:** The book of 2 Kings.

14. **THE PROPHETS WARN ISRAEL AND JUDAH:** The books of 1 & 2 Kings, Ezra, Nehemiah, and from Isaiah - Malachi.

The Exile and Beyond

1. **ASSYRIA SCATTERS ISRAEL:** 2 Kings 17:1 - 18:12.

2. **BABYLON CARRIES JUDAH CAPTIVE.** 2 Kings 24:1 - 25:21; 2 Chron. 36:5-21.

3. **EZEKIEL'S VISION.** The book of Ezekiel.

4. **SHADRACH, MESHACH, & ABEDNEGO THROWN INTO THE FIERY FURNACE:** Dan. 3:1-30.

5. **DANIEL THROWN INTO THE LION'S DEN:** Dan. 6:1-28.

6. **PERSIA OVERTHROWS THE BABYLONIAN KINGDOM:** Dan. 5:1-30.

7. **JUDAH RETURNS TO JERUSALEM:** 2 Chron. 36:22-23; Ezra 1:1 - 2:70.

8. **ESTHER BECOMES QUEEN:** Esther 1:1 - 2:23.

9. **THE PROPHECIES OF HAGGAI, ZECHARIAH, & MALACHI:** The 3 books by those names.

10. **THE SILENT YEARS:** The time from the end of Malachi's prophecy in approximately 400 B.C. until the ministry of John the Baptist.

11. **THE BIRTH OF CHRIST:** Matt. chapters 1 and 2; Luke chapter 2.

FINAL EXAM

1. Fill in all blanks on the map below.

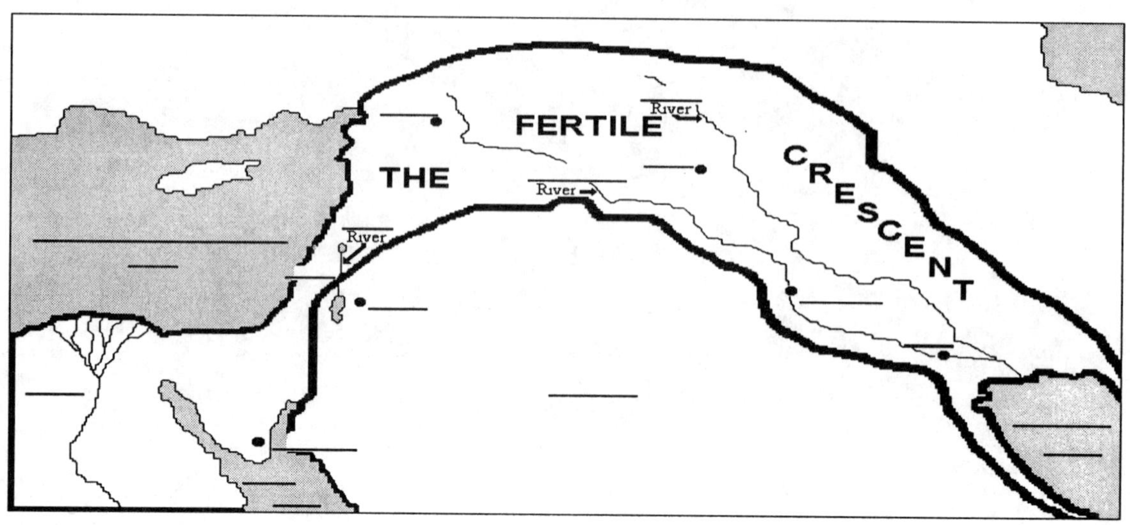

2. Name the **Seven Major Moves** of the People of the Old Testament.

1) E ______________ to ______________
2) U ______________ to ______________
3) H ______________ to ______________
4) I ______________ to ______________
5) E ______________ back to ______________
6) I ______________ to ______________
7) B ______________ back to ______________

3. By categories, list the **"20" Key People** of the Old Testament.

The Six in Genesis

1) ______________
2) ______________
3) ______________
4) ______________
5) ______________
6) ______________

Israel's Eleven Leaders

1) ______________________________
2) ______________________________
3) ______________________________
4) ______________________________
5) ______________________________
6) ______________________________
7) ______________________________
8) ______________________________
9) ______________________________
10) ______________________________
11) ______________________________

The Other Three

1) ______________________________
2) ______________________________
3) ______________________________

4. Where is **the pivotal passage** which gives the plot of the Bible found?

____

5. Identify the **Five Step Cycle** that was repeated over and over during the 400 year period of the Judges.

1) They would ______________________
2) An enemy nation ______________________
3) They would ______________________
4) God would ______________________
5) They would ______________________

6. Compare the **Two Nations of the Divided Kingdom.**

1) N ________	*location*	S ________
2) I ________	*name*	J ________
3) ________	*number of tribes*	________
4) S ________	*capital*	J ________
5) ________	*number of kings*	________
6) ________	*# of good kings*	________

7. In the first column, name the **Three Major Divisions of the Old Testament** and then in the second column give a "simplified" name for each division.

   1) H ______________ or S ________________
   2) P ______________ or S________________
   3) P ______________ or S________________

8. Why are the numbers 17, 12 and 5 significant?

9. In learning the names of the books in the three different divisions, what **alphabetical letter** is significant?

10. Give a good way to remember the basic contents of the following books by filling in the blanks.

    a) The first five words of Genesis are: "_____ ______ ______________ _______ _________." The last five words are: "____ ____ ___________ ____ _______."

    b) Exodus means a mass ____________ or ________.

    c) Leviticus could be referred to as a ___________ ___________ because it gives details for God's plan of worship such as holy days, sin offerings, and other details of the priesthood. It gets its name from the fact that God had singled out the tribe of ___________ as the "priest tribe."

d) The book of Numbers gets its name from the fact that it contains two censuses (or **numberings**) that were conducted 40 years apart — one just after the Israelites left Egypt and the other just before they re-entered the Promised Land. It contains those two ________________ and the 40 years in between that we refer to as _______ _______ _______.

e) Fill in the blanks to show **when** each of the prophets prophesied.

The last three **major** prophets prophesied ______ the Exile.

The last three **minor** prophets prophesied ______ the Exile.

All others prophesied a short while ___________ the Exile.

Politically, all seventeen prophetical books revolve around the emerging and reign of three world powers. Those three world powers are: the ___________ Empire; the _________ Empire; and the __________ Empire.

f) Fill in the blanks to show **to whom** the message of the following five prophets was directed.

J - Jonah ______________________________

O - Obadiah ______________________________

N - Nahum ______________________________

A - Amos ______________________________

H - Hosea ______________________________

g) The message of all of the other prophets was to the nation of ______________________.

11. Name the **Seven Major Covenants** that God made with man.

1) The ______________________________ Covenant
2) The ______________________________ Covenant
3) The ______________________________ Covenant
4) The ______________________________ Covenant
5) The ______________________________ Covenant
6) The ______________________________ Covenant
7) The ______________________________ Covenant

12. Name the **Five Major Time Periods** of the Old Testament and briefly describe each one.

THE FIVE MAJOR TIME PERIODS	
Time Period	***Brief Description***
1.	
2.	
3.	
4.	
5.	

13. Identify the **Key People, Major Moves,** and **Covenants** during each of the **Five Time Periods** and the **Book/Books** where the story is found. (**Note:** Put an * by the name of any of the **Key People** who were also one of Israel's Eleven Leaders or Groups of Leaders.)

BEFORE ISRAEL BECAME A NATION	
Key People 1. 4. 2. 5. 3. 6.	**Book/Books** 1.
Major Moves 1. 2. 3. 4.	**Major Covenants** 1. 2. 3. 4.

ISRAEL IN EGYPT	
Key People 1. 2.	**Book/Books** 1.
Major Moves 1. *(This move was* ***begun*** *during this period.)*	**Major Covenants** *(None of the seven major covenants were made during this period.)*

ISRAEL IN THE WILDERNESS	
Key People 1.	**Book/Books** 1. Last part of ___________. 2.
Major Moves 1. *(This move was* ***in process*** *during the entire 40 years of this period.)*	**Major Covenants** 1.

BACK IN THE PROMISED LAND	
Key People 1. 2. 3. 4. 5. 6. 7. 8.	**Book/Books** 1. 2. 3. 4. 5. 6.
Major Moves *(No major move during this period.)*	**Major Covenants** 1.

THE EXILE AND BEYOND	
Key People 1. 2. 3. 4. 5.	**Book/Books** 1. Last part of ____________ 2. 3. 4. (Also Daniel and Ezekiel)
Major Moves 1. 2.	**Major Covenants** *(**The New Covenant** was **promised** during this period. References to it are also found in other parts of the Old Testament.)*

14. Name the **Fifty Major Events** of the Old Testament.

BEFORE ISRAEL BECAME A NATION
1.
2.
3.
4.
5.
6.
7.
8.
9.
10.
11.

ISRAEL IN EGYPT
1.
2.
3.
4.
5.
6.
7.
8.

ISRAEL IN THE WILDERNESS
1.
2.
3.
4.
5.
6.

BACK IN THE PROMISED LAND
1.
2.
3.
4.
5.
6.
7.
8.
9.
10.
11.
12.
13.
14.

THE EXILE AND BEYOND
1.
2.
3.
4.
5.
6.
7.
8.
9.
10.
11.

NOTES

NOTES

NOTES

NOTES

NOTES

NOTES

NOTES

NOTES

NOTES